IDENTITY

LOST IN HISTORY, FOUND IN PURPOSE.

ASMAHANEY SAAD

Published by **Elevation Publishing Group**
       New York, NY - USA
Cover and Interior Design by **Elevation Publishing Group**

Powered by **Royal Printhood Publishers**
       Kampala - Uganda

Hardcover ISBN: 979-8-9999460-6-5
Paperback ISBN: 979-8-9999460-7-2
E-book ISBN: 979-8-9999460-8-9

In memory of my brother Mohsen Mikidad Saad, aka 'Mickey Ferrari'. I love and miss you dearly.

To all the fallen angels who came before me and shaped my history, this is for your brave stories that remain untold.

PRAISE FOR THE BOOK

"Asmahaney Saad's writing carries a rare mix of clarity, courage, and conviction. This book doesn't confront, reassures, and awakens something in you about who you should be and who you refuse to be. Her voice is powerful and deeply human, offering insights that stay with you long after the last page. I would unreservedly recommend this book to anyone interested in identity, belonging, or the freedom to define one's own path."
-Peace Masiko Hasahya

"Wow, Lost in History, Found in Purpose is a deeply personal and necessary book. It brings out the transformative journey of reclaiming oneself after experiences of systemic loss. Asmahaney projects a remarkably honest and vulnerable voice, articulating the quiet ache of being an "outsider" while carrying a royal, multi-ethnic legacy. Her reflections on courage and resilience are deeply felt. I believe this book would be an essential guide for young women seeking to anchor their worth beyond external validation, showing that purpose is found when you own your full history. Highly recommended for anyone searching for their true center."
-Eng. Kenneth Magembe
Director Armstrong Consulting Engineers

"Identity has always been a topic close to my heart. I've dedicated a lot of thinking to it-written a peer reviewed journal paper on it and even dedicated an entire symposium towards discussions around it. I must admit, I have often thought about Identity as interwoven with cultural heritage, and Asmahaney's beautifully written memoir, challenges this mindset by making the case, her case as is her story, that identity should not always conform to cultural expectations. I see, through her eyes and those of her father, grandfather and others of her heritage that identity is not only a personal anchor but a collective asset that fosters unity, pride, and resilience. In these times of identity dilution, social and political fragmentation, a strong sense of identity can serve as a unifying force that transcends differences and fosters social cohesion. Thank you for this book, Asmahaney and for helping me understand identity more richly."
-Kenneth Muhangi
Advocate
Uganda's Representative at the 4IR, World Economic Forum.

NOTE TO THE READER

Dear Beloved Reader,

Have you ever paused to wonder why you were born and why into the very circumstances, family and history that defined your belonging? Perhaps you have, or perhaps you haven't. Either way, deep within each of us lies a story, one of belonging and identity- waiting to be told. This is mine.

As you turn these pages, you'll discover that my story is just one among many. I count it a blessing to be able to share it because so many stories remain untold. Yet life is made up of stories. They connect us, teach us, and carry the wisdom of generations.

My story is not mine alone. It carries the faces and voices of those who came before me, some of whom I knew personally, while others have been uncovered through this writing journey. Many remain unnamed, but their legacy lives on through every chapter.

This book is a story of hope, and my prayer is that it inspires something within you. It may motivate you to embrace your story and share it with the world. Whether you whisper it to your children or simply write it down for the next generation, So, may you honour your story, because it matters.

As I penned down my thoughts, I often reflected on the greatest book ever written, the Bible. I wondered, "What if those stories had never been told? How would we have met the God we now love? Where would we find the courage, comfort, and truth that shape our lives? That's the power of stories.

So, as you read this book, do not merely see me. Look at it as in a mirror and be challenged and reminded that within you, too, lies a story worth telling.

Thank you for joining me on this journey.

XOXO,

Asmahaney

TABLE OF CONTENTS

FOREWORD

by Olakunle Soriyan aka PK.
Wallstreet Journal, USA Today Best -Selling Forbes Author

So every generation is haunted by a question it cannot escape: Who are we really, beneath the stories others have told about us? Civilizations rise and crumble on the strength or weakness of their answer. Empires wage war over it. Families fracture around it. And individuals (ordinary, extraordinary, and everything in between) are either liberated or imprisoned by it. This book is about this imprisonment; and the rebellion that follows.

"IDENTITY: LOST IN HISTORY, FOUND IN PURPOSE" is an autobiography; but deeper than this, it is a confrontation. A confrontation with the smallness of systems that pretend to own people, the arrogance of bureaucracies that imagine they can reduce a soul to a file, and the inherited blindness of a world that still struggles to understand difference without fearing it.

When Asmahaney Saad walked into a routine passport office, she walked into history. It is a history that has, for centuries, demanded that certain faces explain themselves; a history that has taught institutions to treat complexity as suspicion and heritage as a threat.

What happened to her that day is a simple story of racial profiling, yes; but this is merely the blanket. Underneath this blanket is however the timeless script of power interrogating humanity, demanding documentation before dignifying personhood.

Asmahaney was wounded no doubt; but what strikes me, beyond the wound is the wisdom birthed from it. In this memoir, Asmahaney refuses the luxury of self-pity. Instead, she chooses something far more confrontational: clarity. Shifting away from nostalgia, she goes backward to excavate clarity. She digs into a lineage that stretches across oceans, kingdoms, and centuries: a Yemeni great-grandfather who dared to dream beyond borders; matriarchs rooted in the Bugana Kingdom whose courage predates the nation-state; ancestors who crossed cultures long before colonial maps attempted to define Africa.

Identity, here, is a procession. Her story reminds us that before the colonial state invented the passport, the tribe, or the ethnic box, human beings were already migrating, trading, intermarrying, negotiating cultures, and crafting hybrid identities. She dismantles the lie that identity is meant to be singular, sterile, or easily categorized. Life has never obeyed those rules; only politics has.

Yet, much more than history, the book ends with purpose. What Asmahaney discovers, and what she invites us to confront, is that every human being is carrying three intersecting identities: the one given by ancestry, the one imposed by society, and the one revealed by purpose.

The first is inherited. The second is contested. But the third (purpose) is chosen. It is the only identity that cannot be confiscated, legislated, or denied.

This is where the book transcended the limits of a memoir; and became a manifesto. In rooting herself in Christ, she articulates a truth we prefer to whisper identity is not the final destination; it is rather the beginning of assignment. Identity is the soil; purpose is the harvest; and no administrative office, no racial stereotype, no political category, and no constitutional flaw has the authority to define the destiny of a person aware of their divine calling.

What you hold in your hands is more than a narrative of one woman's struggle; It is a mirror for every nation wrestling with its future. It is a challenge to Africa to confront its own fractures (tribal, legal, historical) and to stop weaponizing difference. It is a call to schools, governments, youth movements, and every institution that claims to shape the next generation: Do not teach identity as confinement. Teach identity as continuity. Teach identity as calling. Teach identity as shared humanity rediscovered.

If we listen, this book offers us a dangerous idea: We are not strangers pretending to coexist; we are relatives rediscovering each other after centuries of misnaming; and relatives, once reunited by truth, do not simply survive; they build.

This book is a gift. A warning. A strategy. A compelling invitation to remember that dignity is not granted by the state; it is inherited from creation.

Also, that what is deserved is a luxury never given nor bestowed; it must be demanded and taken. Read the book slowly. Read it honestly. Allow it to interrogate the parts of you that still believe your worth must be proven to those who cannot measure it.

Ultimately, Asmahaney is not just telling us who she is; she is showing us who we all are; if we have the courage to look beyond the paperwork of our lives and into the purpose that calls us. Do share this book with your loved ones, family and friends. It will be worth their weight in gold and they will each be grateful you did. Enjoy.

Olakunle A. Soriyan

Fall, 2025.

By: Olakunle Soriyan PK

ACKNOWLEDGEMENTS

First and foremost, I thank God whose divine wisdom, mercy, and faithfulness have carried me through every step of this journey. Without a life rooted in Him, none of this would have been possible. It is for His glory that I write and share this book.

I am deeply grateful to the people who have walked this path with me, those who prayed for me, encouraged me, and believed in me even when I struggled to believe in myself. Writing this book has been one of the most challenging and vulnerable experiences of my life. But God, in His goodness, placed the right people around me for a time such as this.

To my church family at House of Revival Church (HOR), and to my pastors, Michael and Esther Kintu; thank you. Pastor Michael, when I first arrived at HOR, I carried brokenness and questions. Nonetheless, you saw beyond that and boldly declared a great destiny over my life. Your words became a turning point, and I am forever grateful.

To the Disciple and Leadership Ministry at HOR in which I serve, thank you for fostering an environment of growth and purpose. Dr. Tony Hasashya and the entire team, your encouragement was crucial in helping me uncover my story and step into it with boldness.

To my editors, Ms. Shubrah Claire Kasozi and your dedicated team at Royal Printhood Publishers, thank you for your patience, professionalism, and the care you brought to this process. You helped bring structure, clarity, and heart to every page. To my friend Nathan Kiwere, thank you for your insightful review of this book.

To Dr. Daniel Ruhweza, your wealth of wisdom has contributed mightily to this book. Thank you for the invaluable time and input you so graciously offered. Special appreciation also goes to Norbert Katfigazi, my researcher for accompanying me on this writing journey and helping me uphold clarity and truth.

To Zohair Kasim and family in Canada, thank you for sharing your family's story and contributing to this book.

A special honor to my mentors, coaches, and encouragers who have shaped my journey: _ Henriette Paula Mugisa, I recall one conversation that lit the path to writing not only this book but a trilogy- I am still marveled! Thank you for your wisdom and the laughter we shared in the process.

To Mr. Patrick Ayota, your wisdom and thoughtful guidance have helped shape my journey in a quiet yet lasting way. Like many other life strategies, you taught me to develop, this book would never have reached the international market if it weren't for your challenging thoughts.

To Engineer Kenneth Magambo and the Soaring Eagles cluster, Mr. David Kabiswa, and Dr. James Magara, thank you for a year of transformational learning through the Oakseed Governance Programme.

To my Partners at KTA Advocates, thank you for your consistent support and encouragement. Kenneth Muhangi, your early belief in this project gave me the courage to carry it through.

To the United Bank for Africa family, Next Media services, Epssom Energy, the Ministry of Finance and all the spaces that have shaped my career and given me the opportunity to grow my acumen in leadership, governance and business-thank you!

To my father, Haji Mikidad Saad, thank you for your openness, your stories, and for trusting me to tell our family story.

To my mother, Riziki Katende, thank you for your courage and willingness to share difficult parts of our history.

To my uncle, Farooq Abdalla Foum Katende, thank you for helping me recognise what I had overlooked in my own story.

Special thanks to my husband, Godfrey Tomusange, and our children, Ayden Shein and Amar'e Sherman Tomusange. You are my heart. Thank you for listening, encouraging, and reminding me why this book matters. Your love gives me strength.

Saving the best for last, to you, my dear readers, thank you for opening yourselves to these words of truth shared from my heart.

PROLOGUE

In 2021, as the world grappled with the COVID-19 pandemic, the Ugandan Government continued to oversee the implementation of its directive issued in 2018 for all citizens to replace their old passports with a new East African passport, a step towards easing the free movement of people within the East African Community (EAC). As a citizen deeply invested in the EAC integration process, I wholeheartedly embraced this initiative. With a straightforward online application process, I began doing this for myself and my family; I paid the fees and secured an appointment at the immigration office.

On a crisp Monday morning, just two weeks after our submission, we arrived early at the immigration office. Seated in the crowded pews, I felt prepared, documents in hand, as I waited for our turn. When we were finally called, I walked confidently to the counter with my children, expecting a routine procedure.

However, the routine check took an unexpected turn when the immigration officer looked at me and asked, "Where are you from?" Accustomed to such questioning because of my distinctive appearance and unique name, I responded with a calm smile, "I am Ugandan."

"Which part of Uganda?" she pressed further.

Pausing briefly, as my patience started to run out, I replied, "Kasese."

"But people from Kasese don't look like you," she retorted skeptically.

"And what do they look like?" I asked politely, my tone still steady.

"They just don't look like you," she dismissed.

I directed her to my file, pointing out that this was my fourth time renewing my passport. Moreover, my passport had not yet expired, but I was complying with the government directive. I reminded her that my first passport was issued during my university years, with my father's backing, and I assumed my records were intact.

Despite presenting my valid national identification card, which clearly confirmed my citizenship, she focused on my appearance rather than my documented identity, claiming a system upgrade had wiped my records.

The situation escalated when she questioned my tribe, suggesting that perhaps I was a Munyankole, not a Mukonjo from Kasese. I corrected her firmly, "I am a Mukonjo, from Kasese. My grandfather, born in Yemen, moved here in the 1900s and married a Mutoro, which grounds my father's identity in Uganda."

Her relentless probing heightened the insult, and she suggested a language test in Rukonjo, a dialect I did not speak, having been raised and educated in Kampala. The absurdity peaked when, amidst this bureaucratic nightmare, my young sons, having witnessed the entire episode, expressed their confusion and fear, sensing the overt hostility.

This interaction painfully reminded me of an earlier ordeal in 2003 when I was travelling to Nairobi for an inter-university event as part of the Makerere University Students' Guild Association. Upon arrival at the Malaba border between Uganda and Kenya, I was detained. Mistaken for Somali or Rwandese, I was pulled aside and taken into a small, dimly lit room where I was subjected to harsh interrogation by the immigration officers. Despite my repeated pleas and insistence that I was Ugandan, their response was one of disbelief. "How did you end up with a Ugandan passport?" one officer sneered. "You must be Somali, Eritrean, or Rwandese. We Ugandans don't look like you. Even your name, it doesn't sound Ugandan!"

Their tone was accusatory, and their manner was cold. My voice trembled, but I persisted in trying to explain. Still, their suspicion remained unwavering. It was only after a desperate, tearful phone call to my father that things began to change. He spoke to one of the officers in *Rukonjo* and *Rutoro* (local dialects from Western Uganda) and confirmed my heritage. As it turned out, one of the immigration officers recognized the names of my grandfather and father, and the legacy they left in Kasese. He was visibly embarrassed. My father reminded them that by now, the Saad family from Kasese and the diversity we represent should be well known. Only then, after a grueling hour or so, was I finally allowed to continue my journey to Nairobi.

Overwhelmed by a mixture of sorrowful emotions, I silently vowed that day never to travel to Kenya by road again. To this day, I have kept that vow. It was a genuinely traumatic experience.

Fast forward, here I was, standing before this immigration officer, yet still within my homeland's borders, feeling as if I had been thrown back into that nightmare.

The officer proceeded to deliver her prejudiced verdict; my sons would receive their passports, thanks to their father's Baganda heritage. As for me, I was told to either return with my father or submit to an interview in Rukonjo, and if I failed, it would mean that I hadn't sufficiently proven my Ugandan citizenship. I firmly reiterated my previous stance, that I would not be calling my father for an interview as I believed I was a fully-fledged Ugandan adult woman with every right to be at the office, and should not be subjected to the embarrassment of having to call my "daddy" every time my identity is questioned.

I was stunned, not only by the ignorance of the law but also by the blatant discrimination displayed by this immigration officer. During their training, they would have been instructed to set aside personal bias and treat everyone with fairness and professionalism.

Frustrated and deeply hurt, I walked away, but the damage was already done. What hurt even more was the presence of my children. They stood there, listening, watching, and absorbing every word. At that moment, I felt a profound sense of helplessness and embarrassment.

I returned to work feeling broken, weighed down by the thought: How do I seek justice? The next morning, I woke up with renewed resolve. I realised that my most powerful weapon was the knowledge of my rights under the Constitution and Laws of Uganda.

So, I sat down and began to write, detailing my experience in a formal letter addressed to the Ministry of Internal Affairs, through the Minister and the relevant administrative officers. I narrated my harrowing experience and demanded accountability and respect for my rights. This incident, echoing past injustices, reaffirmed my determination to advocate for myself and others facing racial, ethnic, or other forms of profiling.

Unbeknownst to me, the Ministry's response to my letter was to send a team to my ancestral village of Bwera in Kasese to investigate my heritage. A few days later, my father called, puzzled as to why government officials were at our home in Bwera, asking questions about me and my connection to the Saad family. He had assumed that I was getting a 'big government job' and that these people had come to conduct a background check as part of the due diligence process. It was at that point that I shared the whole experience with him. He was equally offended that such incidents continued to trouble his children. He empathised deeply and assured me of his full support in whatever course of action I would take.

Boosted by his support, I started to seriously think about legal action against the Government, aiming to get a court intervention that would deliver justice not only for myself, but also to help prevent this injustice from continuing for future generations.

Shortly after, a former classmate from law school, now working in the Ministry's legal department, contacted me. She acknowledged my letter, apologised for what I had endured, and confirmed that the actions at the immigration office had resulted from sheer ignorance. S

he also informed me that my passport and those of my children had been approved and were ready for collection. I went to retrieve them at the earliest opportunity.

At that time, I had already begun my pursuit of justice. However, upon making further inquiries, I discovered that a similar case had already been filed in the High Court by members of the Somali and multiracial communities in Uganda. Their case challenged the unconstitutional denial of their right to receive national identity cards, as well as other discriminatory acts in contravention of their Ugandan citizenship, perpetrated by officers of the Directorate of Citizenship and Immigration Control and the National Identity Regulatory Authority (NIRA). After speaking with one of the petitioners, Mr. Yasin Nasher, I sadly learned that the case had already reached the judgment stage, meaning it was no longer possible for me to be added as a party.

Ultimately, I chose the path of personal healing. I decided to move on, rooted in the truth of who I am, supported by my family, and determined never to let my identity be questioned or diminished again.

I realised that this experience was not pointless. It marked a turning point, a painful yet essential step in my journey to understand my identity beyond the constraints of laws, borders, and bureaucracy. It became the start of a deeper quest: to reclaim self, dignity, and purpose for myself and for all who have ever felt deprived of their rightful place in the world.

Reflecting on my experience with Uganda, I realise the profound impact understanding one's heritage can have in confronting racial profiling and bias.

This experience was not merely a personal inconvenience but a sobering reminder of the widespread challenges many face due to superficial judgments and systemic issues. It highlights the importance of equipping oneself with knowledge about one's roots and history. As readers turn the pages of this book, I hope it motivates them to explore their own backgrounds, strengthening their identity and resilience against prejudice — or ignorance.

I envision a society where this knowledge closes gaps, fostering understanding and inclusivity. Through this narrative, I also encourage introspection on constitutional protections and societal norms, advocating for a future where no individual has to endure what I did. My journey from humiliation to self-assertion is shared to comfort anyone who has ever felt different, while also sparking a collective call to action that ensures our stories drive societal progress and legislative reform

PART I

The Ancestral Thread

> *"A people without the knowledge of their past history, origin, and culture is like a tree without roots."* — *Marcus Garvey.*

This is my Genesis story. From my father's Yemeni heritage to my mother's roots in the Buganda Kingdom, and the moment their paths crossed—this is how I came to be. These are the roots that birthed Asmahaney Saad

Chapter 1

The Beginning

To understand the forces that have shaped my journey, including the challenges I face today and the strength I draw from within, I must take you back to where it all began: my family's history. Mine is a story woven through generations and across continental borders. As I started to learn about these early lineages, a sense of belonging and purpose started to bud, even in a world that often sought to define me by labels. As I heard about their stories, I found that I inherited not just a name but a legacy, one that gave me the resolve to rise above prejudice and to press forward with conviction.

A YEMENI ADVENTURER

My great-grandfather, Sayyid Mubarak, was born in Yemen in the late 1800s. At that time, Yemen was a centre of Islamic scholarship, trade, and cultural exchange, connected to East Africa through the emerging trade routes. Drawn by the opportunities offered by the prosperous East African coastal trade and possibly enticed by the youthful call of adventure, Sayyid Mubarak decided to leave his homeland.

He sailed across the Gulf of Aden and eventually settled in Somaliland. This region was under the influence of the British Empire. This bold choice marked the beginning of a new chapter that would shape our family history.

He was a businessman who traded goods such as garments, ostrich feathers, ghee, and other animal products. While living and trading in Somaliland, my great-grandfather found love and later married my great-grandmother, Amina Sayyid, who came from the Marehan clan, one of the prominent clans in Somaliland at the time. Together, they began their life journey; my great-grandfather was a Yemeni adventurer, and my great-grandmother was a Somali native born and raised on African soil. They later started a family, which included my grandfather, Saad Bin Sayyid.

My grandfather, Mzee (respectful title given to elders) Saad Sayyid, was born in Kismayo in the late 1800s during British colonial rule. Later, the area became part of Somalia after the British divided the region during the renowned scramble and partition of Africa, which involved European powers dividing up their African colonial territories. As a young boy, my grandfather moved frequently with his father, who was always travelling for trade. Later, as conflicts in the region increased—particularly with the arrival of different colonial powers such as Italy, France, Germany, Egypt, and others—my great-grandfather decided to move the family inland to what is now Kenya.

Eventually, my grandfather settled in Kenya, and later, in the early 1900s (as I am told), he moved to Uganda as a young man full of entrepreneurial dreams and ambitions.

He began by working for an Indian family involved in the cotton business in Budaka, a town in Eastern Uganda. Later, he opened a cotton store and built many connections. One of his closest friends and business partners was a man also named Sayyid Mubarak (not to be confused with his father). Together, they later relocated to Mbarara, in Western Uganda, to seek new business opportunities.

My grandfather became a successful cotton farmer and was known for encouraging people in Budaka not to leave their homes to work on colonial farms. He believed people could succeed by working their own land instead. Many who followed his advice ended up doing much better than those who left to work for the foreigners.

My grandfather, according to my father's narration, often spoke reverently about his father, my great-grandfather Sayyid Mubarak. These stories depicted an honest man who valued family and never cowered in the face of adversity. My father later told us how his grandfather eventually returned to Yemen later in life for unknown reasons. Whether it was a nostalgic call to what was once his homeland, a yearning for the land of his birth and the familiar cadence of its language, or a desire to reconnect with the family members he had left behind, or perhaps a decision born of personal reflection towards the end of his years. Whatever the real motivation, it was never clearly expressed, and we are left to wonder. From the fragmented tales I have heard, my great-grandfather likely died in the early 1910s and was buried in Yemen.

A Land of Opportunity

Mzee Saad Bin Sayyid, my grandfather, was born in Kismayo, Somaliland (Kenya), to my Yemeni great-grandfather, Mzee Sayyid Mubarak, and my Somali great-grandmother, Amina. Due to the division of colonial borders, the region later became part of Somalia. My grandfather was born during the early British colonial period (late1800s), when the East African British administration ruled Somaliland. Later, the British divided Somaliland and transferred control of the area to the Italians.

Mzee Sayyid arrived in Uganda during the early days of the British colonial era in East Africa. It was a perilous time marked by significant ongoing migration driven by border divisions. In the late 1910s, he first visited Budaka in the Busoga region of Eastern Uganda, where he channelled his entrepreneurial spirit into establishing a prosperous cotton business. His ambitions soon led him westwards. In the 1920s, he relocated to Mbarara in the Ankole region, and later to Kabale. It was in Kabale that he met his first wife, Fatuma, a Ugandan woman of Rwandese heritage, with whom he welcomed his firstborn, Mohamed Saad.

The allure of opportunity drew him further during the salt boom of the 1930s in Western Uganda. Recognising the economic potential, my grandfather made the pivotal decision to relocate to Kasese, a thriving frontier town on the rise. My grandfather aspired to engage in salt mining at Lake Katwe which is located in Kasese, and he later opened a salt store and began trading exclusively within the Kigezi, Ankole, and Rwenzori regions.

Not long after, he moved to Bwera-a neighbouring town which borders the Democratic Republic of Congo, where he bought a plot of land and built his first shop, symbolising his deepening roots in Uganda. Amidst the lively cross-border trade and cultural exchange, my grandfather found more than just business success. He also gained brotherhood. He formed a close friendship with Juma Twafiki, a respected Islamic teacher and community leader in Bwera. Their bond was strengthened not only by their shared faith but also through mutual respect and their commitment to Islamic values.

Twafiki introduced him to Mzee Hamisi, my maternal great-grandfather. Their friendship grew strong, bonded by religion and a shared interest in business and community development. Eventually, Mzee Hamisi married his daughter, Zaituni Bint Hamisi, to my grandfather. Together, my grandparents had five children: Amina Bint Saad Sayyid, Kassim Bin Saad Sayyid, Faisal Bin Saad Sayyid, Ramla Bint Saad Sayyid, and my father, Mikidad Saad Sayyid. Sadly, their other sister, Leila Bint Saad Sayyid, died of measles at the age of five. Mzee Sayyid's family further expanded through subsequent marriages in Islam: he married Mariam Bint Iddi from Katwe as his second wife, with whom he had two children; then Bichea Saad Sayyid, his third wife, who bore two other children; and finally, his fourth wife, Mugenyi, a Mutooro from Kamwenge Fort Portal, who gave birth to a son, Abdul Bin Saad.

Mzee Sayyid's business acumen extended well beyond retail and trade; it boldly ventured into the agricultural frontier at a time when few recognised its full potential.

With a visionary mindset, he pioneered farming ventures, particularly focusing on the cultivation of pawpaw and coffee. These crops later became key sources of economic empowerment in the region. He was among the first in Bwera to recognise the commercial viability of these crops, especially pawpaw, whose water extract began to gain popularity in European markets during the 1950s and 1960s.

Seizing this opportunity, he mobilised and mentored local farmers, encouraging them to embrace pawpaw farming not just as a subsistence activity but as a profitable enterprise. He organised training sessions, facilitated access to seedlings, and advocated for better post-harvest handling practices to meet the standards of the export market. His efforts quickly transformed Bwera into a hub for pawpaw cultivation, bringing increased income and economic vibrancy to the area.

At the same time, he expanded into coffee farming, recognising the long-term export value and stability it could provide. His leadership during this flourishing economic period was not only entrepreneurial but also rooted in the community. He promoted the idea that collective prosperity was more significant than individual gain. As a result, his initiatives did more than increase household incomes; they inspired a generation of farmers, fostered a spirit of innovation, and left a lasting impact in Bwera.

Later, Mzee Sayyid moved his operations from Bwera to the capital city, Kampala, seeking broader opportunities for both business and family. He settled in the suburb of Kisenyi, where he bought a modest residential house whose door was always open, not just for family, but for friends and community members in need of guidance or help.

Until his passing in October 1972, my grandfather remained a unifying force within our family. He upheld the values of hard work, integrity, and generosity. Inspired by his example, the family resolved to keep his spirit alive by not only continuing the business ventures he had started but also by investing in the social well-being of the community.

In his honour, they established institutions like the Saad Memorial Secondary School in Kiburara, Kasese district and the Rwenzori Saad Islamic Institute in Bwera, each serving as a testament to his lifelong commitment to education, faith, and empowerment.

Roots and Legacy: Mzee Saad Sayyid

Narrated by Haji Mikidad Saad Sayyid (my father a.k.a. Daddy)

My father, Mzee Saad Sayyid, was not only a businessman but also a deeply God-loving and God-fearing man. He built his life and trade on a foundation of honesty and integrity. His business centred around the buying and selling of cotton, but what truly set him apart was his unwavering commitment to truth and justice. Dishonesty had no place in his dealings, and he lived by the values of sincerity and fairness, qualities that were clearly visible in everything he did.

On one occasion, he advised local farmers not to sell their cotton to dishonest Indian traders known to cheat them. He also directly confronted the traders, urging them to be honest in their business dealings. Unfortunately, his advice was ignored. As the exploitation persisted, Mzee Saad took a courageous stand: he led a farmers' strike against the Indian traders. Under his leadership, the cotton farmers collectively refused to sell their produce to those who cheated them.

His actions caused ripples in the trading community. The Indian traders, feeling pressured, reported him to the District Commissioner, accusing him of organising the strike. Summoned to a meeting, Mzee Saad stood his ground bravely. He explained how the farmers were being misled, both in the weighing of cotton and in the payments received. He argued that unless the Indian traders practised fairness and transparency, the farmers would continue to withhold their cotton. He remained steadfast for justice and gained the respect of many.

His advocacy did not end there. When tea plantations were established in Fort Portal, white settlers began forcefully recruiting labourers from Bwera and the surrounding regions. Mzee Saad vehemently opposed this form of exploitation. He would travel as far as the Gombolola (sub-county) to intercept and help people escape from trucks transporting them to the plantations. He discouraged such labour, referring to it as slave work, and instead motivated people to work for themselves. His message bore fruit: those who heeded his advice often prospered, while many who had left returned disillusioned. Those who returned frequently embraced his wisdom and went on to build successful lives.

Mzee Saad was a liberator, fearless in the face of injustice. He challenged both colonial powers and the exploitative Indian merchants who saw Africans as cheap labour. He was relentless in his pursuit of fairness, dignity, and empowerment for his people. Beyond his activism, he was a generous and compassionate man. He wanted everyone to live with dignity. He encouraged people to dress well, often lending clothes to farmers who could repay him after the harvest season. He promoted agricultural development, urging the community to grow cash crops such as Arabica coffee and papayas to improve their livelihoods.

Mzee Saad's influence also extended to education. He played a crucial role in developing education in Bukonzo. He was key in rallying the community to establish several important schools: Mpondwe Muslim Primary School, Bwera Primary School, Karambi Primary School, and Kyarumba Primary School. As a founding member of Mpondwe Muslim Primary School, he also acted as an education agent for the Government. In this role, he would personally pay teachers on behalf of the Tooro local government and later be reimbursed. This was a period when teachers were scarce and resources limited. Nonetheless, he remained dedicated to ensuring education reached the community.

His work in education was strengthened through his partnership with the Muluka Chief, Ramadhan Karangai. Together, they championed both farming and education.

They mobilised the community to grow food crops like maize and cassava alongside cash crops, establishing a sustainable foundation for community development. Mzee Saad even invested in a maize and cassava milling machine, which he used to produce flour supplied to Kilembe mines and the tea plantations.

Reflecting on the legacy of the Saad family and the numerous contributions my grandfather made to his community, it is astonishing to consider that it all commenced with a single act of courage. First, my great-grandfather, Sayyid Mubarak's decision to leave Yemen was the initial spark of a long, unfolding story. He ventured into the unknown, crossing borders in pursuit of opportunity and adventure.

Later, it was Mzee Sayyid, my grandfather who took that dream even further. His bold decision to settle in Uganda was a significant act of faith. In a land unfamiliar to him, he carved out a new home, started a family, built a business, and most importantly, dedicated his energy to uplifting those around him. Through his generosity and vision, he became a pillar in his community.

That single journey laid the foundation for what we now know as the Saad family: a legacy founded not just on personal success but also on the values of integrity, hard work, and compassion. It is a legacy that has positively touched many lives and continues to motivate the generations that come after.

Tracing our ancestries, we do more than honour those who came before us; we reclaim parts of ourselves that history may have buried. Each story, name, struggle, and triumph in our lineage carries whispers of identity that shape how we see ourselves and the world around us.

Understanding our history empowers us to walk with greater purpose. It anchors us in something deeper than titles or achievements; it grounds us in legacy. As we forge our own paths, we begin to see that identity is not a mask we wear, but a map we follow, from origin to becoming. To know who you are, you must know where you come from. In knowledge, there is unstoppable power.

Chapter 2

The Matriarch's Thread

There comes a moment in every person's life when inner truth must be acted upon externally. In those instances, identity is not only recognised but also tested, validated, and developed. Then arises a call of duty to explore that crucial point where personal conviction intersects with divine purpose, and where understanding who you are requires more than knowledge; it demands responsibility.

Throughout history, those who truly discovered their identity were often called to something greater than themselves. Moses could not stay in Pharaoh's palace once he knew he was Jewish by blood. Queen Esther could not remain silent in the comfort of the palace once she knew her voice was meant to save a nation. Jesus Himself, as the Son of God, declared, "For this cause I was born…"

This chapter raises important questions: What duty is your identity calling you to? What purpose were you created to fulfil? Embracing who you are involves accepting a divine assignment—a mission uniquely made for you. When the call of duty arrives, may you be prepared—not just aware of your identity, but fully living out its purpose.

A Unique Blend: Fumu-Katende Legacy

No history is complete without recounting the stories of women who have shaped us, and my mother's lineage exemplifies that truth. My maternal grandfather, Abdallah Fumu, was the son of Fumu Jimba, who was born in the Comoros Islands. Fumu Jimba was the son of Mzee Msehendo, who was the son of Mzee Fumu (*Msa'fumu*), a Sultan of Grand Comoro, now known as the Comoros or Comoro Islands. Mzee Fumu (*Msa'Fumu*) led a rebellion against French colonial rule and was executed for his involvement. He descended from the noble Bafumu lineage and was widely recognised as *Mzee Fumu wa Bafumu*.

This heritage of resistance and sovereignty shaped my grandfather, Abdallah Fumu. A British soldier and later a registered veteran of the British army, his life's journey would intersect with another powerful lineage, one from the Buganda Kingdom in Uganda.

The Bow That Would Not Break: A Legacy of Resilient Women

On my great-great-grandmother Asha's side, the family's roots extend deep into the Buganda royal court. Asha's mother, Nambi, was a Muganda woman of royal descent. She was the only daughter of Kaweke, a descendant of Kibagulo Elyabalema Ssese, who in turn descended from Tebuseke Ndugwa, a notable elder of the Lugave clan.

Ndugwa had seven children, and from this lineage emerged my great-great-grandmother, Nambi Kaweke, a strong and intelligent woman destined for a unique life.

Nambi was raised in the Buganda royal palace by her aunt, Rehema Ndagire, who was a 'lady' of the court under Kabaka Mutesa I, the King of Buganda in the 18th century. Later, succeeded by Kabaka Mwanga II, his resistance to the British Colonial power led to a very volatile and eventual fall of his reign. After his defeat, Kabaka Mwanga II fled to

Germany East Africa (modern day Tanzania) and was later exiled to Seychelles where he died.

Nambi my great-great-grandmother like many of his subjects, after the fall of his reign, were captured and exiled across East Africa-she was specifically exiled to Northern Sudan. Due to her royal status, even as a captive, she was somewhat shielded; she was neither enslaved nor discarded. Instead, she was married off to Sultan Salim Bilal Bay (Salim Bay), a high-ranking Nubian military commander associated with the Ottoman Empire. They had sixteen children together.

Not long before they could lay a proper foundation, war in the Ottoman territories compelled the family to flee. They eventually settled in Nakuru, Kenya, in an area called Eldarma Mavine which is a town in present day Baringo County in the Western part of Kenya. There, Salim Bay died and was buried. Following his death, Nambi, resilient as ever, asked her only surviving child, a daughter, Asha Bilal Bay, to accompany her back to Uganda.

Upon her return, Nambi shared her story with Nuhu Mbogo, a royal of the Buganda Kingdom. Her life's journey, from palace upbringing to Ottoman exile and back, I have been told were documented and archived under the title "Ebyafaayo bya Nambi" (The Memoirs of Nambi). These records remain in the historical library of the Kingdom, preserved under the lineage of Nuhu Mbogo, Kakungulu, and Prince Nakibinge.

Back in Uganda, Nambi (my great-great-grandmother) and her daughter Asha settled in Mbale, in a government reserve called Nakibiso. Asha (my great-great grandmother later married Dr. Ali Talabali, a Pakistani doctor brought in by the British during the construction of the East African Railway. Together, they had eighteen children. After Talabali's passing, Asha continued to live with her mother, Nambi, and her children (including my grandmother Zena), and they later relocated to Kampala. Nambi and Asha both died of old age and were laid to rest in Kampala.

A Love Beyond Heritage

My grandmother, Zena Talabali, once shared the story of how she met my grandfather, Abdallah Fumu. She mentioned that their first meeting happened during visits to Kibuli. There was a man called Mzee Mtajazi who often hosted guests, especially from Comoros and Zanzibar. My grandmother frequently visited Mtajazi's home because her cousin was married to Mtajazi's brother. During one of those visits, Mtajazi introduced her to Abdallah Fumu. That is how they became acquainted.

When Zena, my maternal grandmother, asked about his profession, my grandfather told her that he was a soldier who had arrived with the British soldiers. He was a marine trainer responsible for training marine soldiers. Besides this role, he was one of the engineers who worked on Bugolobi Flats (then known as the Marine Houses). He also served as one of the supervisors in the construction of the Ugandan Parliament. He lived in Naguru, not far from his workplace.

After some time, my grandmother accepted him and took him home to introduce him to her parents. That's when the traditional engagement took place. He was given conditions for marriage: he would have to accept that their children would live with her family and adopt the Lugave clan (one of the prominent seven Nansangwa or original clans in the Buganda Kingdom).

After two months of courtship, Zena and Abdallah Fumu married in Kibuli, at Mtajazi's residence. To this day, a place called Mtajazi Stage is named in his honour. Their marriage in the 1950s united two powerful traditions: one of East African royal bloodline and the other of Comorian noble. Interestingly, my grandfather's second-born son (MHSRIP), Iman Abdalla Katende, later married a daughter of Mtajazi as well. Both my grandparents, Zena (Nambi) and Abdallah (Katende), were respected and fully integrated into the Buganda Kingdom. Their children, and by extension my generation and I, carry the Lugave clan name with deep reverence.

We are descendants of warriors, scholars, and queens. From Mzee Fumu of Comoro, who defied colonial rule, to great-great- grandmother Nambi of Buganda, who crossed empires and returned to reclaim her identity, to Asha, the matriarch who held our legacy together through faith and family, we come from a line of strong, enduring women and men of purpose.

What happens when love transcends borders? When it surpasses skin colour, culture, or tribe. For a man like my grandfather Abdallah to choose to join a different tribe and adopt a new family line out of love demonstrates the power of love. When love genuinely speaks, it breaks down barriers. It creates new eternal bonds. From 'Fumu' to 'Katende', a path was chosen. This was not because he wished to abandon his noble Comorian roots. Instead, he decided to connect his story with another, both equally significant in their own right.

The matriarchs in my lineage were not just queens because of their bloodline, but because they held their heads high in the face of great tribulation. Whenever I feel discouraged, I think of my great-great-grandmother Nambi, who went through exile and found her way home. Her story gives me strength. If she could survive that, then I can face whatever mountains life throws my way. This is what it means to stand on the shoulders of those who came before me.

It is the realisation that I do not walk alone. Every step I take is imbued with the strength of our ancestors. I am their wildest dreams, unanswered prayers, and unfinished stories, now brought to life through me. I come from greatness, not just in title, but in truth.

Breaking Barriers

Narrated by: Farooq Abdullah Fumu (my maternal uncle a.ka. Uncle Farooq)

On the face of it, growing up as a child of mixed heritage living in Buganda was not challenging for us. This is because we were born in Uganda among the Baganda community. Our mother was a Muganda of Pakistani-Nubian origin, while my father was an assimilated Muganda of Comorian-Omani origin. Growing up, we didn't face many difficulties because we spoke both Kinubi and Luganda. It wasn't until we went into exile that we met our Pakistani relatives from my mother's side. But even then, we still considered ourselves Ugandan. We continued to speak Luganda and Kinubi (a Sudanese-Arabic dialect), but not the Pakistani language because we were unfamiliar with it.

The issue of identity as a child of mixed heritage was a common relationship challenge, not a matter of citizenship. The primary identity issue we faced was simply being Baganda, despite our lighter skin. We constantly had to explain ourselves. Most of the community members who knew us recognised us as one of them. With the Nubian community, we didn't experience segregation, but there were instances of bullying. We learned to cope with that because we were deeply rooted in Buganda. We had descendants there, and we were accepted and recognised as part of the community.

Navigating passport and citizenship issues by law is relatively straightforward. Other people might face difficulties, but within my local community, I am recognised as one of their own—a Muganda by tribe. When I applied for a passport, I was interviewed and shared my lineage, which was accepted. I was granted a passport. My origin is Uganda, and I am a Muganda by tribe from the Lugave Clan. In fact, my Luganda is better than that of many grandchildren of the current Baganda and others!

Reflecting on my parents' lives, they were Muslims and took pride in their faith. My father wasn't tied to any specific tribe but genuinely loved the Baganda culture. He often spoke with deep respect and admiration for the Kabaka, mainly because he lived through the era of the 1969 overthrow and beyond. He was a sincere, peaceful man who was deeply fond of the Lugave clan. He particularly advised us to understand that we were Baganda, born of Baganda and the Lugave Clan. He made it clear that we would grow up here and live in Uganda, our country. My grandmother was also a true Muganda woman. She loved everything about the Baganda way of life. She was conservative in her behaviour and strong in her values. She raised us with discipline, taught us respect, and always reminded us to live as responsible members of the Buganda community and proud Ugandans who love their country

The story of my maternal grandparents, Zena and Abdallah Fumu Katende, is not just a tale of love, it is also a window into an older world, one that looked at belonging differently. In kingdoms like Buganda, Bunyoro-Kitara, and Tooro, identity was fluid yet founded in communal values. A stranger could arrive with nothing but goodwill and through marriage, friendship or service, they could be embraced as part of the community. The act of assimilation was not seen as dilution of identity, but rather as expansion and enrichment.

Those who integrated were given local names and added to the existing clans. A 'Fumu' could become a 'Katende' not by abandoning their past, but by joining their future with that of their new family. It was a system anchored in human connection rather than documentation; one where Ubuntu mattered more than credentials.

Sadly, much of that changed with the arrival of colonial structures. The systems of registration, identification, and classification reduced identity and belonging to paper and ink. Belonging became something to be verified. To date, even marrying into a community is not always enough to be accepted. What was once sacredly human has become bureaucratically superficial. We no longer ask, "Who has joined us?" but "Where do they come from?" The spirit of integration that once defined us has dimmed under the weight of systems that taught us to see difference as division.

And yet, the story of my grandparents reminds me that all is not lost. There is still a possibility for love to override paper and ink. A possibility for true belonging to exist beyond registration. This can only be born in the willingness to connect, to understand, and to love across boundaries.

Chapter 3

Connecting the Dots

Every story has a beginning. Mine starts long before I was born, within the lives of two people whose worlds could not have been more different, yet whose paths crossed in a way that still feels, even now, like divine choreography. My mother, Riziki Abdalla Fumu Katende, was the eldest of the five children of Zena Talabali and Abdallah Fumu, born on 21st July sometime in the late 1950s. She grew up in Mengo, then a quiet suburb but now part of Kampala's central business district, in a conservative and close-knit Muslim family. Her early years were spent between home and schools like Nakivubo Blue Primary, where her education commenced.

My father, Haji Mikidad Saad Sayyid, was born in the 1940s in Bwera, Kasese, the fourth of thirteen children in the Saad family, recognised for its strong Islamic heritage and notable business stature. Beyond Kasese, his reputation extended in both commercial and religious circles throughout Uganda.

The way my parents met is one of my favourite stories to hear from my mother, partly because of its simplicity and partly because of how it influenced the rest of our lives. She was on her way to secretarial college when my father first saw her at a bus stop. He was already a successful businessman, driving his Mercedes-Benz to a meeting, when his eyes met hers. Later, he would describe her as "angelic." He rolled down the window and offered her a lift. Although she hesitated, his respectful and calm manner persuaded her to accept. That ride led to another, then another, until daily pick-ups grew into companionship. Not long after, he approached her father to formally ask for her hand in marriage.

On 22nd August 1976, at fifteen (*a socially acceptable age for marriage during that time*), my mother became his wife. Coming from a conservative Muslim background, marrying a man of his standing was seen as an honour for her family and a promise of security for her. To her younger self, it felt like stepping into a dream.

Marriage introduced her to a life she had never imagined. Almost overnight, she was exposed to the world of travel, accompanying my father to Kenya. Additionally, she visited Belgium, France, and other European cities she had only read about. For a young woman raised in a modest Ugandan setting, these trips were truly breathtaking. It wasn't just about staying in luxury hotels or sightseeing; it was about experiencing new cultures, foreign languages, and different ways of life that ignited a spark within her. She returned from each journey with her world slightly broader and her confidence somewhat greater.

My mother was the second of the three wives my father married, in accordance with Islamic practice. Together, they had six children, including my siblings and I. However, we were part of a much larger family with twenty children spread across three households.

I was born to my mother Riziki Katende, and father Mikidad Saad, on a quiet Sunday afternoon, 12th December 1982, at Nsambya Hospital in Kampala, Uganda. For many years, there was lingering uncertainty about my exact date of birth. My mother, perhaps overwhelmed by the labour and the hazy blur of those hours after delivery, often wavered between the 9th and the 12th of December. It wasn't until later on in my adult life that I decided to retrieve my official hospital birth records that the date was finally confirmed: 12th December 1982.

I am the 4th born among my mother's children, but the 14th among my father's twenty children from his 3 wives. According to my mother, carrying me during pregnancy was surprisingly smooth; there were no alarming symptoms or major discomforts, and hardly any complications. However, while the pregnancy may have been uneventful, my arrival into the world was anything but. The labour was long and gruelling and was characterised by a tense atmosphere in the delivery room.

I was born weighing a substantial six kilograms, considerably above the average for a newborn. Due to certain medical risks related to my birth, the doctors immediately placed me on oxygen therapy. I was closely monitored and subjected to a series of tests to rule out any underlying complications or health issues.

Although my mother was exhausted, she later told me that seeing me breathe steadily and respond to touch brought her great relief.

In those early years, my father made a conscious effort to provide well for us. We lived in Muyenga, one of Kampala's wealthiest suburbs, surrounded by my mother's extended family and her circle of loyal female friends who became aunties in every sense. It was a village in the truest sense, where child-rearing was shared and love and discipline flowed from many hands.

In the early 1980s, political instability compelled our family to move to Kenya. My memories of that period are faint, but my mother's stories create a vivid picture. We first lived in Plainsview Estate, then in Golden Gate Estate in Nairobi, adapting to new routines and cultures. When the National Resistance Army now Movement government came to power in 1986, my parents decided to return to Uganda. My older siblings joined Buganda Road Primary School, while I began at Kampala Kindergarten.

Growing up in a polygamous household had its richness, with a constant hum of activity and a sprawling mix of siblings, cousins, and relatives, but it also had its quiet aches. I often felt invisible in the crowd. More than material comfort, I longed for an intimate bond with my father. I envied my friends' stories of bedtime stories, school drop-offs, and cheers at sports days. My father's presence was more symbolic than constant. His life was divided among three homes and many children, along with an even wider circle of young people he mentored. His love was something I had to piece together from brief conversations or formal greetings. As I grew older, that emotional gap between us only widened.

My father was a man of ambition, managing businesses across Kasese, Kampala, Nairobi, and Zaire (present day Democratic Republic of Congo). The weight of his responsibilities began to take its toll. One by one, his ventures faltered, and the strain seeped into our home. The entrepreneurial zeal that had once lit his eyes faded, replaced by quiet exhaustion.

It was during that period that a radical shift in my mother's life took place. She transitioned from being a housewife to becoming part of family's financial well-being. She began by renting out part of our William Street property, which was evolving into a busy commercial hub. Later, she ventured into running a salon and selling fashionable kitenge fabrics and accessories. It was a transformation that filled me with awe. Gone were the silk dresses; in their place stood a woman with calloused hands, unwavering determination, and the resolve to keep her children in school no matter what.

Her steadfast belief was that education was the great enabler. She never had the chance to complete her own, as marriage ended her schooling at fifteen, but she was determined that we would not share that fate. She committed herself to our academic lives, attending school meetings, supporting co-curricular activities, and building strong relationships with our teachers. Through the grace of God and her relentless effort, all six of us earned university degrees, and I went on to achieve two master's degrees, one in International Business Administration and the other in Oil and Gas Management.

That was her victory, not a title or wealth, but breaking a cycle. As I raise my own children, I follow her example, prioritising my presence at every stage of their growth.

By the time I was finishing high school, my parents' relationship had reached breaking point. Divorce, though culturally frowned upon, became inevitable. For us children, it was disorienting. My father's withdrawal after the separation was complete. Without a word, he disappeared from our lives, leaving no calls, no letters, and no presence at birthdays. Even when I invited him to my wedding, hoping for reconciliation, he refused to attend, rejecting my choice of a Christian spouse.

In the years that followed, I realised how tough life could be without a parental safety net. My friends couldn't relate to the instability I had experienced. Without a mentor or trusted guide, I withdrew behind emotional walls. Survival became my sole focus. Trust felt perilous. Rebuilding that trust has been one of the most difficult journeys of my life. It hasn't been straightforward, but I continue to move forward. I've learnt that healing is slow, but every small step counts.

Ultimately, our stories are more than just memories; they serve as maps. They reveal where we come from, what has shaped us, and what we must decide to carry forward. My mother's resilience, my father's complexities, the absence, the presence, the pain, and the lessons all form part of the compass that now guides me.

PART II

Forgotten Facts, Stolen Futures.

> *"Injustice anywhere is a threat to justice everywhere." — Martin Luther King Jr.*

Instead of protecting the people, the law has sometimes been weaponised as a tool for exclusion and erasure.

Chapter 4

The Land, the People and the Name

I have always wondered where we truly begin. Not the names on our birth certificates, not the tribes people recite when they introduce themselves, but the place before all of that. The time before the world decided what to call us. I imagine the land as it once was, alive with its own pace, a place where belonging came not from documents or declarations but from the soil beneath your feet and the community that claimed you as theirs.

One of my earliest understandings of migration came through my mother's stories about our years in Kenya during Uganda's political unrest. I was far too young to remember all the details, but she would tell me how our family quietly packed up in the night, leaving familiar faces behind. She spoke of the relief of safety mixed with the unspoken realisation that, even though Nairobi was not new to her, we were there as people in exile.

Neighbours were kind, yet there was always that gentle but undeniable reminder that we were living on someone else's land. That tension between warmth and distance stayed with me long before I could grasp the history that shaped it.

Before there was a Uganda to call by name, there was land—ancient, untamed, and rich with stories. People lived in harmony with the seasons, guided by memory and tradition rather than constitutions or national anthems.

To speak of identity here is to go deeper than modern labels. It is to see it rooted in the soil, the sky, and the communities that lived in harmony with both. Understanding this earlier world, its customs, values, and ways of belonging, helps peel back the layers that time, politics, and colonial borders have added.

We live in a world defined by borders, lines drawn to separate countries, regions, tribes, and classes. These boundaries influence politics and access to resources, but they do not exist in the human heart. Beneath the surface, we are all travellers—curious and restless, always seeking meaning, safety, and belonging. This urge to move is ancient. From the first human migrations out of Africa, people have crossed deserts, oceans, and mountains in pursuit of survival, trade, adventure, or the hope of something better.

Whether through the Bantu migrations across Africa, Viking voyages through Europe, or Polynesian journeys across the Pacific, movement has shaped every civilisation.

No land has ever been home to a single people forever. Every group, no matter how rooted it now appears, arrived from somewhere else.

Before colonial rule, the area now recognised as Uganda was already attracting human settlement. Bantu-speaking farmers and ironworkers began arriving from Central Africa around 1000 BCE, settling in the south and west. They introduced new crops like bananas and millet, the craft of iron smelting, and systems of organised governance that laid the groundwork for strong kingdoms such as Buganda, Bunyoro-Kitara, and Ankole.

From the north came Nilotic-speaking pastoralists such as the Acholi, Langi, Iteso, and Karamojong, with herds, age-grade leadership systems, and clan-based social structures that remain strong today. Later, the Luo arrived and intermingled with northern communities, influencing their governance and customs.

These migrations were not always peaceful. There was competition for land and resources, but also trade, intermarriage, and alliances that intertwined diverse traditions. The clan system served as a bridge, integrating newcomers into local communities by assigning them clan identities or recognising shared ancestry. This facilitated cultural blending without erasing origins.

Uganda's landscapes, from Lake Victoria's shores to highland farms and wide savannah, supported farming, fishing, herding, and metalworking. Trade routes linked the region to what is now Kenya, South Sudan, Rwanda, and the Democratic Republic of Congo. Long before Europeans arrived, Uganda was integrated into larger networks of trade and culture.

Colonial rule disrupted these natural patterns. Migration became linked to economic exploitation and administrative convenience. The British recruited and sometimes forced labour from inside Uganda and neighbouring Rwanda, Burundi, and the Congo to work on plantations, railways, and roads. Certain groups, especially the Baganda, were preferred for leadership roles under indirect rule, while others were limited to hard labour.

My father often spoke about this period, recalling how some of our extended relatives were drawn into colonial-era labour migration. They would leave home for months at a time to work on coffee plantations or construction sites far from their villages. He remembered how they would return leaner, their hands scarred, and their native Swahili and Arabic dialects mixed with new words from the languages of the people they had worked alongside. Those journeys were not just about earning wages; they changed how people dressed, spoke, and saw the world. Even without passports or visas, migration left its mark on identity.

Colonial policies intensified ethnic identities, using them as administrative categories in censuses, taxation, and governance. Communities that had once blended over time were now labelled and ranked, laying the groundwork for post-independence mistrust and political rivalry.

Migration, however, has always been about adaptation as much as movement. In the pre-colonial era, migrants introduced farming techniques, new livestock breeds, and trade connections that enriched local economies. Under colonial rule, migrant labour was vital for cash crops like coffee and cotton, as well as for building the infrastructure that connected the country.

These stories tell of the hardships that different people had to endure in their quest for movement. Migrants faced displacement, instability, and exclusion from political participation, even when they had contributed significantly to Uganda's development. Refugees, whether Polish families during World War II, Indian traders, or neighbours fleeing regional conflicts, encountered both opportunity and rejection here.

Colonial border-drawing during the Scramble and Partition of Africa at the conference in Brussels in 1886, created more problems, splitting ethnic groups and blocking traditional migration routes. Kingdoms like Buganda were divided, changing settlement patterns and breaking up cultural identities. Trade also shifted from barter systems and slave routes to cowrie shells and Indian Rupees, which were introduced through the Indian Ocean and caravan trades. Strategic kingdoms like Buganda became busy trading centres, attracting merchants and workers from across East and Central Africa.

Today, Uganda's migration story continues. Government policies, such as the Comprehensive Refugee Response Framework, aim to integrate newcomers. Still, challenges persist in resources and political will. Migrants continue to navigate a system that does not always meet their needs.

For me, this history is more than just academic; it resonates deeply with my personal experiences of identity and belonging. Ethnic profiling, stereotypes, and the subtle but persistent currents of tribalism in Uganda are not new. They are echoes of centuries-old migrations, colonial favouritism, and political manipulation.

Growing up, I often felt the weight of how my name, my tribe, or the assumptions people made about my heritage could influence the way I was treated. Sometimes it was subtle — a change in tone, an unspoken judgment, or cautious politeness. Other times, it was straightforward — as if I had to prove my belonging. It taught me that ethnicity here is not merely about heritage; it is connected to history, power, and perception.

Understanding Uganda's migration story has given me a different perspective. It reminds me that no one's claim to belonging is purer than another's, and that each of us comes from people who once crossed a border, entered new territory, and learned to make it home. It has made me slower to judge and quicker to see connections where others might see differences.

We can remember that our shared story is one of movement, adaptation, and integration. In that case, we can begin to imagine a Uganda where belonging is not inherited by bloodline but earned through contribution, compassion, and the will to live together in peace.

The following testimony, by my father, Haji Mikidad Saad, provides a firsthand account of how migration, politics, and ethnic identity intersected during Uganda's most turbulent decades.

Haji Mikidad Saad Sayyid- A Legacy of Service

I was born in Bwera and began my education at Mpondwe Muslim Primary School. Later, I joined a private school and progressed up to Primary 8, Junior Secondary. After completing my education, I joined my father's business, marking the beginning of my entrepreneurial journey.

As a young man, I observed the political development of Uganda. I recall the political parties of that era, especially the Uganda People's Congress (UPC) under Prime Minister Milton Obote, and Sir Edward Mutesa as President. In 1971, Amin took power, ruling until 1979, when he was ousted by the FRONASA forces led by His Excellency the President of Uganda, Yoweri Kaguta Museveni. The turbulent political scene persisted with the contested 1980 elections, leading to the liberation movement and the eventual takeover by the National Resistance Army (NRA) under Yoweri Museveni in 1986.

During these chaotic times, my business was severely impacted by looting and instability. In search of safety, I fled to Kenya, where I continued my business pursuits while engaging with political figures committed to Uganda's liberation. In Nairobi, I met individuals aligned with Museveni's vision of peace and stability for Uganda. I offered ideas and material support to the liberation cause. Among the influential figures I interacted with were Dr. Crispus Kiyonga, Dr. Ruhakana Rugunda, and Mathiri Kakire. Together, we discussed ways to restore peace and constitutional stability in Uganda.

I aspired to become a member of the General Assembly to help stabilise Uganda's constitution. However, my attempt to stand in Busongora South was unsuccessful, as tribal sentiments favoured my opponent, Mbusa Muhindo.

45

Despite my commitment to unity and development, my non-Mukonzo identity hindered my political ambitions.

Despite political setbacks, I remained committed to community service and was eventually accepted by the Rwenzururu Kingdom. The Kingdom, led by Rumangoma and his father, acknowledged the contributions of the Saad family to the Bakonzo community. As a result, I was elected as the Member of the Rwenzururu Kingdom Parliament representing Mpondwe Rubiliha Town Council. My primary role was to promote unity and advocate for peace within the Kingdom.

I strongly identify as a Ugandan citizen, emphasising that my family's decision to settle in Uganda made it our permanent home. I married a Ugandan, raised my family in Uganda, and firmly believe in honouring and valuing one's roots.

I emphasise the importance of education, advocating for the enlightenment of the younger generation to understand their history and build a better future. I also emphasise the significance of respecting religion and recognising the world's transient nature.

Reflecting on my life, my greatest regret is succumbing to unverified rumours and tribalism, which harm unity and progress. I advise others to steer clear of hatred and gossip, as these are destructive forces that impede community development and harmony. I hope to be remembered not for my faults but for my positive contributions to my community and my steadfast spirit in both difficult and victorious times.

Such personal histories enrich our understanding of migration's impact on identity, grounding it not in abstract movement but in lived experiences of resilience and adaptation.

Today, Uganda continues to experience complex and dynamic patterns of migration and integration. These movements are driven by numerous factors, including population pressure, economic opportunity, conflict, and cultural exchange, all of which transform communities and identities in enduring ways.

The Bakiga, for instance, traditionally lived in the highlands of Kigezi, but have migrated in large numbers over recent decades due to land shortages. Many have settled in places like Fort Portal, adjusting to new environments and intermarrying with local communities such as the Batooro. This has led to blended cultural practices, shared kinship ties, and shifting identities that challenge strict ethnic boundaries.

Uganda has also seen a notable influx of South Sudanese nationals, many of whom have fled conflict or sought better socio-economic opportunities.

Their presence in both urban centres and refugee settlements adds another layer to the country's already diverse cultural fabric. In places where South Sudanese and Ugandans live side by side, new forms of integration emerge through shared education, commerce, religious practice, and intermarriage.

As people continue to move, blend, and establish new homes, ethnic distinctions that were once clear are becoming increasingly fluid. Belonging to a particular tribe is no longer solely defined by bloodline or birthplace but also by upbringing, social connections, and shared experiences.

These changes are evident in evolving perceptions of ethnic stereotypes. For example, older generations may have described a "typical" Muganda woman as short, stout, and broad-featured. However, today one might just as easily encounter a tall, light-skinned woman with very different features who still identifies strongly as Muganda. Her identity is confirmed not only by her language and customs but also by her role within the community.

Such evolving identities remind us that culture is never static. It adapts, absorbs, and redefines itself with every generation. Uganda's story illustrates how mobility, intermarriage, and shared spaces are reshaping the ethnic landscape, softening old boundaries and creating new forms of belonging.

Migration has always played a central role in Uganda's history, from the ancient Bantu migrations and Nilotic movements to colonial-era resettlements and contemporary refugee flows. It has woven a rich tapestry of cultures, languages, and traditions, but it has also created tensions. During the colonial period, migration was often manipulated as a tool of control. Ethnic groups were categorised, ranked, and strategically positioned, sowing seeds of inequality and suspicion. These divisions were later reinforced by post-independence politics, where ethnicity was politicised for power and influence.

Ethnic profiling in modern Uganda cannot be separated from this history. The casual assumptions, the coded language, the invisible barriers created by someone's name, language, or origin are legacies of centuries of migration and the political systems built around it.

Understanding migration patterns and their implications is not merely an academic exercise. It is personal. It involves reclaiming the narrative, confronting stereotypes, and challenging inherited hierarchies. It serves as a reminder to reflect on how history persists in our present and to envision a future where ethnicity is not a tool for exclusion but a thread in a shared national identity.

Before there were borders, flags, or colonial names on maps, there was land, alive with memory, rhythm, and spirit. It was not only inhabited but deeply known. People moved in harmony with seasons, spoke languages born from the soil, and held identities shaped by belonging rather than imposed labels.

This chapter reminds me that identity is not just what others call me but what has always been mine, what has always been carried in my story, rooted in my ancestry, and preserved across generations. Long before the world tried to define me, I existed, thrived, and named myself in the identity of the countless people that came before me. To truly understand who we are, we have to look beyond the names and rediscover our origin. And origin is not about geography, it concerns memory, dignity and the power to rediscover lost narratives.

As I learnt about and reconnected with the land before the name, a truth deeper than history was uncovered, one older than conquest, stronger and more powerful than any name on a map. That there is more to our history than what meets the eye.

I had always tried to fit into diluted narratives, but along the way, important parts of my identity were stripped away as I tried to fit into boxes that were already defined for me.

Going on this journey of identity has been my way of piecing myself back together—of remembering who I have always been.

Chapter 5

The Making or Breaking of a Nation

Who was Uganda intended for? At the very inception of the Republic, what vision did our constitutional forefathers hold when they set out to define the essence of this nation? It is high time we faced these questions and the danger of allowing one man's narrow view of identity to shape the meaning of citizenship and belonging.

I was not alive during Idi Amin's regime. However, I have read, listened, and reflected enough to understand the deep scars it left, especially on Ugandans of Asian descent. Their suffering serves as a warning of what can happen when leadership is based on exclusion, fear, and prejudice.

Today, we live in an era of many silent Amins. These are not military rulers making public declarations, but individuals who quietly hold the same dangerous beliefs about who qualifies as Ugandan.

They sit in offices, churches, boardrooms, classrooms, and even family gatherings, making decisions and shaping opinions through the lens of race, tribe, or religion. This quiet prejudice can be more dangerous than open hostility because it conceals itself in plain sight. If such a person were to rise to power again, cloaked in populism or posing as a saviour, Uganda could regress into the same blood-stained history of the 1970s.

This is why I wrote this chapter. With the guidance of constitutional law experts like my esteemed colleague Dr. Daniel Ruhweza and the voices of those who lived through that period, I aimed to capture not only the legal and historical truths but also the emotional and social costs of exclusionary politics. This is not about reopening wounds. It is about disinfecting them before they fester and infect future generations.

A Uganda for "ONLY" Ugandans?

In August 1972, President Idi Amin Dada shocked Uganda and the world by ordering the expulsion of more than 80,000 people of South Asian descent, mostly Ugandan citizens of Indian and Pakistani heritage. They were given 90 days to leave. The announcement, made abruptly on national radio, was framed as a step towards restoring economic independence and empowering indigenous Ugandans. In reality, it was state-led ethnic cleansing that uprooted families, destroyed communities, and redefined the meaning of citizenship.

Amin justified his decision by accusing Asians of hoarding wealth, refusing to integrate, and sabotaging the economy. He claimed God had instructed him to remove "economic saboteurs."

Behind the religious claim was a political calculation. Faced with inflation, rising dissent, and unrest, Amin saw the Asian community as an easy scapegoat. The move garnered short-term popular support from some indigenous Ugandans while distracting the public from the regime's failures.

Many of the expelled Asians were Ugandan citizens by birth, registration, or naturalisation, protected under the 1967 Constitution. Yet they were stripped of their citizenship overnight, their passports revoked, and their homes and businesses seized without compensation, with their rights nullified without due process. The Departed Asians Property Custodian Board was established to oversee the management of vacated assets. However, instead of safeguarding them, it distributed the assets to political loyalists, soldiers, and civil servants who often lacked the skills or the willingness to maintain the businesses.

51

The consequences were quick. Businesses collapsed, supply chains disintegrated, and unemployment rose sharply. Uganda's economy, which had depended heavily on the skills and networks of the Asian community, spiralled into decline.

The Rupture of a Nation

The policy did more than expel people from their property. It tore them away from their identity and sense of community. Many had lived in Uganda for generations, contributing to its economy, culture, and social fabric. They spoke local languages, celebrated Ugandan customs, and regarded the country as their only home.

Expelled families dispersed across the globe, moving to the United Kingdom, Canada, India, Australia, and Kenya. Resettlement was often difficult. They navigated immigration procedures, faced racism, and rebuilt their lives from scratch. The loss was not only material; it was the heartbreak of leaving ancestral graves, places of worship, and the streets where their children had played.

For children and youth born in Uganda, the shock was even more intense. They had sung the national anthem with pride and never thought they could be perceived as anything other than Ugandan. Being suddenly labelled as "stateless," "refugee," or "exile" inflicted emotional wounds that would endure for decades.

Back in Uganda, schools, hospitals, and factories once operated by Asians were understaffed or left abandoned. Lacking the expertise to manage the redistributed properties, many businesses failed. Urban centres like Kampala, Jinja, and Mbale lost their economic vitality. Infrastructure deteriorated, and the multicultural balance of communities broke down.

The expulsion redefined who was considered Ugandan. Citizenship became linked to ethnicity and race rather than legal status or shared national identity. This deepened suspicion of minorities and undermined Uganda's diversity.

The mindset persisted beyond Amin's rule. Even after his fall in 1979, communities of Rwandese, Congolese, South Sudanese, and Somali descent often found themselves in limbo… present in Uganda but never fully accepted.

They encountered obstacles in obtaining identity cards, owning land, and accessing services. Prejudice endured not only in government systems but also in attitudes passed down through generations.

A Call for Reconciliation

After Amin's fall, Uganda faced the tough challenge of repairing the damage. In the 1980s and 1990s, President Yoweri Museveni's government encouraged expelled Asians to return and reclaim their properties. This created tension with Ugandans who had occupied those properties for years. Legal disputes and political sensitivities made restitution a slow and complicated process.

The 1995 Constitution marked a turning point, affirming property rights in Article 26 and expanding the definition of citizenship in Articles 9 and 10. By the early 2000s, many Asian-Ugandans had returned, reviving businesses and once again contributing to the economy.

Yet reconciliation remained incomplete. Some families chose not to return, having built new lives abroad. Those who did come back found a country that had changed socially and economically, and acceptance was not always assured. The trauma of the past continued to influence how they were perceived.

The Day We Lost Everything - Zohair Kassim

My great-grandfather, Alarakhia Kassam, left India for East Africa when he was about 13 to 15 years old. He travelled with a friend, and according to family accounts, they may have snuck onto a ship to make the journey. They arrived in Mombasa and then travelled inland, sometimes hitchhiking and sleeping on trains, until they reached Uganda.

Once in Uganda, my great-grandfather worked odd jobs in shops before managing to open his own store. Later, despite having no prior experience, he began farming and purchased land. Over time, he bought additional properties and sent for his siblings to join him in Uganda.

By the time my grandfather, Ebrahim Alarakhia Kassam had my father and his siblings—3 daughters and 4 sons, the family lived in Kololo, in a home that was now turned into a school. The house was near the mosque and cemetery, which were central to my great-grandfather's daily life. My father, Zulfikarali Ebrahim Kassam, attended Nakasero School. All was progressing well; my family had built a successful life in Uganda until the infamous directive was issued on 4th August 1972.

From what I've been told by my father, his siblings, and even my late grandfather, the expulsion of Asians from Uganda was swift, surreal, and yet, somehow, not surprising.

Like so many other families, they were given just two weeks to leave. Fourteen days to pack up their entire lives. My grandfather, Ebrahim Alarakhia Kassam had already renounced his British protectorate passport by then, choosing to embrace a Ugandan identity.

So when the order came, they were left with only Ugandan passports in their hands, and suddenly, those meant nothing. They were stateless, unwanted… persona non grata in the only country they called home.

For my father Zulfikarali, it was overwhelming. He had just been admitted to study abroad in England, one of the first in his family to get that opportunity. My grandfather was going to let him go, but the timing couldn't have been worse. As the two-week notice ticked down, his departure date approached, and my grandfather had to break the news: you're not going anywhere until we know what's happening to this family. Everything was put on hold. Survival came first.

What was strange to them at the time was how calmly my grandfather seemed to take the news. He had warned them years before: "Prepare for a day when we lose everything." He had seen the signs, read the political weather forecast. The businesses, the land, the house, they were never as permanent as they seemed. He knew it and had tried to prepare his children for the storm ahead.

One story that stayed with me is what happened on the plane as they left. One of Idi Amin's generals had apparently threatened my grandfather, saying if he found out he was on the flight, he'd either have the plane turned back or, worse, shot down. My grandfather had supplied eggs and produce from his farm to senior officials, maybe even Amin himself. He was also an acquaintance with Ben Kiwanuka, the then Chief Justice of Uganda. He was not just some distant stranger to the regime. He had reason to be afraid.

So when they finally boarded that flight, there was a weight in their hearts heavier than any suitcase they had carried along.

So great was their trepidation that when the pilot's voice came over the intercom and said, "We've left Ugandan airspace," my father and his siblings cried. Not from relief alone, but because those words confirmed what their father had told them all along. This is the day everything was gone.

In that moment, they realized they weren't just leaving behind land and buildings. They were losing a whole life. A future. A certainty. A home.

Rebuilding in a New Land

My family's journey after the expulsion did not end when the plane left Ugandan airspace. It was only the beginning. While my father and his siblings cried on that flight, realizing their worst fear had come true, they had no idea just how much would be asked of them next.

They spent a year in a refugee camp in Austria, waiting to be relocated. Brazil was on the table at one point, but in the end, Canada welcomed them, thanks in large part to the Aga Khan of the Ismaili community's ties to then Prime Minister Pierre Elliott Trudeau.

That is how my family ended up in Ottawa, then Toronto. My grandfather, once a landowner and respected farmer in Uganda, was reduced to hard manual labour, working the land with his own hands in a small town outside the city. It broke him, not just the work itself, but the indignity of being treated as though he had never built anything, never belonged anywhere. Friends from the community who had already arrived from Kenya and Tanzania came to visit him, saw the toll it was taking, and helped him move to Toronto to start over, again.

It wasn't just the struggle to find work. It was the racism, the constant reminders that they were outsiders. My father told me how people would spit at them in the street, calling them names, telling them to go back. But where, exactly, was "back"? My grandfather had given up his British protectorate passport. Uganda had rejected him. And Canada, though it offered refuge, did not feel like home.

By the time my father became a young adult in Canada, he had managed to carve out a path through education. He studied electronics and computers, adapting, evolving. However, the wound of exile never really healed. Uganda lived in his memory as a place of both love and loss. For years, he did not go back, and I think part of him didn't let himself belong anywhere fully. There was always the fear that home could once again be taken away.

When he finally began returning to Uganda many, many decades later, something surprising happened. He began to feel... different. Comfortable, even. Perhaps not "at home" in the way he once was, but not a stranger either. On the other hand, I grew up in Canada with the story of exile written into my family history. But in the last year alone, I've visited Uganda three times. And each time, I have felt more welcome than I could have imagined.

The Homecoming

I remember the moment clearly. July 2024. We had just landed at Entebbe Airport. My father went through passport control first. Then I approached the immigration officer. He asked what I was doing in Uganda, and I explained I was there with my father for family matters. I told him my father was born in Uganda, but I was Canadian.

He looked at me and said, "If your father was born in Uganda, then you're Ugandan. You're one of us." That wasn't the only time I heard those words.

During one of my visits, a Ugandan nurse in an ambulance looked at us with disbelief when we told her my father was born in Kampala. When she heard about my grandfather, and even great-grandfather before him, she paused and said, "So you're from here."

Again—an Uber driver, upon hearing my story, smiled and said, "You're more Ugandan than I am." It was a recurring theme. The people I met didn't just acknowledge my roots. They embraced them and embraced me.

I've traveled to many countries; the Middle East, Europe, North America, but I can say without hesitation that Uganda is one of the most welcoming places I've been. Not just because of hospitality, but because of something deeper. A recognition. A reclaiming.

Today, I don't say Uganda is my home in the legal sense. I was born in Canada. I live there. But Uganda is my homeland. It is where my family's story stretches back generations, and where strangers tell me, without hesitation, "You are one of us."

Notably, Uganda's expulsion of Asians was sudden and explicitly racialised. Her neighbor, Tanzania under Julius Nyerere also nationalised Asian businesses, but did so gradually within a socialist framework. Kenya experienced many Asians departing due to restrictive policies and anti-Asian sentiments, but there was no large-scale expulsion. South Africa's apartheid-era removals were severe but carried out within a legally established racial hierarchy.

Uganda's sudden purge undermined the rule of law and breached international human rights, leaving it isolated on the global stage. The economic collapse that ensued was a direct result of prioritising political gain over inclusivity.

A Cautionary Tale

As I reflected on the events of 1972, I realised that they were more than just a socio-economic disaster. They represented a brutal rewriting of national identity, one that fractured families, shattered trust, and displaced the very feeling of home for thousands.

This could easily have happened to my own family. But from what I have been told, the nature of their assimilation in both Kasese for my paternal family and in Buganda for my mother's family offered a kind of shield. Because of my paternal grandfather, Mzee Saad Sayyid's deep involvement and contributions to the community in Bwera and Kasese, he was widely accepted as one of them.

On the other hand, my maternal grandfather Abdallah 'Fumu' Katende and his family had already registered as Ugandan during the colonial period and had adopted Baganda identities and names that became part of who they were. They found protection in that assimilated belonging. My grandmother even went as far as taking in several people, claiming them as relatives to safeguard them from the turmoil that unfolded.

It is undeniable that Uganda has made strides toward healing; through legal reforms, restitution, and attempts and reconciliation. However, the shadows of the past still linger. What I have come to understand is that identity is not a privilege for the state to bestow or revoke. It is something built slowly, through shared lives and contribution. When it is denied, the damage extends far beyond the immediate loss of livelihoods; it creates generational wounds of alienation that do not easily fade.

The real lesson is clear. Nations must guard against leadership that defines belonging through exclusion. True unity is not achieved by drawing lines but by erasing them through empathy and inclusion. And for those who choose to identify with a new people or place, that choice must come with the willingness to fully embrace that identity, just as the spirit of assimilation once allowed families like mine to remain recognized as Ugandan.

Chapter 6

Uganda

A Nation of Many Faces

Contributed by Dr Daniel Ruhweza

In every nation, beneath the esteemed symbolism of flags, borders, and anthems, lies a quieter, more personal question: Who truly belongs?

On paper, citizenship is about documents and legal status. However, it is much more personal; it is connected to our sense of self, our place in the world, and our right to be recognised. It shapes our identity, sense of belonging, and the power we hold as a "people". It determines who can claim state protection, whose voice is heard in its decisions, and whose story becomes part of the nation's shared memory.

In this chapter, we go beyond birth certificates and passports to explore the essence of citizenship. We look at how history, politics, race, ethnicity, and class come together to decide who is included in the "party" and who isn't.

From the shadows of colonial rule to today's intense immigration debates, from refugees seeking safety to indigenous peoples protecting ancient lands, and from stateless children to distant diasporas, the question remains urgent: Who has the authority to decide who belongs, and what justifies their judgment?

We will examine the legal frameworks and cultural narratives, while also considering lived experiences. We will analyse the contrast between how citizenship for some is granted at birth as a gift they never needed to request, while for others, it is a prize fought for over years or a fragile status that can be revoked without warning.

More than that, however, this chapter invites readers to look beyond paperwork, to question the invisible borders in our minds, and to confront the truth: citizenship is not just a legal category. It is a battleground—one where the struggle is not only for inclusion, but also for dignity, equality, and the right to belong.

Citizenship, Identity and the Law

Understanding the complex relationship between citizenship, identity, and law in Uganda requires a thorough examination of the country's constitutional framework and its historical background. The legal system concerning citizenship in Uganda is not only a result of modern governance but also influenced by colonial history, ethnic diversity, and changing legal ideas of belonging. Today, the question of who belongs in Uganda, who is a citizen, who has the rights and duties of citizenship, and who is excluded from that category, remains a key issue, especially for multiracial and multiethnic citizens.

Uganda's Constitution establishes a legal framework that recognises various classifications of citizenship. However, the law does not explicitly address multiracial or multiethnic identities using those terms.

Instead, it introduces several categories of citizenship based on an individual's connection to Uganda, whether through birth, registration, naturalisation, or foundling status. While these classifications enable a diverse population to claim legal belonging, they also reflect a society that is complex and sometimes divided along ethnic and national lines.

Citizenship by birth is the most straightforward form of legal belonging. This category includes people who are born within Uganda's borders or those born to Ugandan parents. However, there is a significant distinction here regarding who is considered "indigenous." The Constitution recognises certain ethnic groups as indigenous, or nationalities, whose members are granted citizenship by birth. This distinction, which is outlined in Schedule 3 of the Constitution and clarified in Article 10, carries significant implications for individuals from certain groups, as it ties their citizenship directly to their ethnic roots.

However, the issue becomes more complicated when considering foreign nationals who marry Ugandans. Citizenship by registration, for example, allows foreigners who marry Ugandan citizens to acquire citizenship. For instance, imagine a person from Saudi Arabia who marries a Ugandan citizen. By virtue of the marriage, they would qualify for citizenship by registration. Yet, this type of citizenship is far more tenuous than citizenship by birth. If the marriage is found to be fraudulent or if the individual engages in actions detrimental to the state, such as joining a rebel group, Ugandan law allows for the revocation of citizenship by registration. This presents a significant vulnerability for individuals whose citizenship is based on legal procedures rather than birthright. Even if a person has been married for years, should the state deem the marriage invalid or should they engage in political actions it deems treasonous, they could lose their citizenship.

A further complication arises with citizenship by naturalisation. This form of citizenship is available to individuals who have resided in Uganda for an extended period and wish to formally adopt the country as their own. However, like citizenship by registration, naturalisation involves risks. For instance, if a naturalised citizen engages in activities that undermine Uganda's sovereignty, such as committing any treasonous act, they can lose their citizenship. This process signifies a recognition of loyalty to the state, and if that loyalty is compromised, citizenship can be revoked. This underscores the provisional nature of non-birthright citizenship in Uganda, highlighting the legal gap between those born in Uganda and those who acquire it later, and illustrating the fragility of citizenship that is not inherently linked to one's ethnic identity or historical presence in the country.

Then there is the category of foundlings, which is one of the more unique and potentially controversial forms of Ugandan citizenship. The law grants citizenship to any child under five years old who is found abandoned in Uganda, with no known parentage. This ensures that abandoned children are protected under the law, but it has also raised concerns about possible abuse. In theory, an individual could deliberately abandon their child, leaving them to be found and automatically granted Ugandan citizenship under the foundling clause. This creates a loophole that could be exploited for political or personal gain, exposing a flaw in Uganda's citizenship laws regarding the protection of the system's integrity.

While these classifications allow for various paths to citizenship, the Constitution also outlines a set of duties for citizens under Articles 10, 12, 13, and 14. Citizenship in Uganda is not merely about rights; it also involves responsibilities. Citizens are expected to fulfil certain obligations, such as paying taxes and participating in national duties like voting.

Thus, citizenship is a form of inclusion, where one is not only granted access to certain privileges but also expected to contribute to the welfare and functioning of the state. This framework reflects an attempt to bind individuals to the state, ensuring that all those who belong legally to Uganda also participate in its development.

Despite this inclusive framework, Uganda's citizenship laws still bear traces of colonial-era legal structures. The British colonial administration left a lasting impact on Ugandan legal and political systems, and one of the most persistent legacies is the 1926 cut-off date used to determine who is considered a citizen by birth. Under the colonial system, anyone not found within the borders of what is now Uganda by 1 February 1926 could not be recognised as a citizen by birth. This colonial decree defined who was indigenous and who was not, creating a legal boundary that did not reflect the cultural and ethnic realities of the people living within these borders. This arbitrary marker still influences Ugandans today, even though it was designed to serve the interests of the colonial state.

For example, this system has posed significant challenges for ethnic groups that span national borders, such as the Maasai. The Maasai people have traditionally been nomadic, moving freely between Uganda, Kenya, and Tanzania. However, under modern national borders, their legal status as Ugandan citizens become complicated. A Maasai individual born in Uganda might experience different legal treatment compared to a Maasai born in Kenya or Tanzania, despite sharing the same cultural and ethnic identity across these borders. This division highlights a much larger issue: how the borders established during colonial times do not reflect the realities of ethnic and cultural identity.

Similarly, in regions like West Nile, communities that share cultural and linguistic ties with people across the border in the Democratic Republic of the Congo (DRC) or Sudan find themselves in a vulnerable position. These communities may see themselves as part of a larger ethnic group that crosses the political borders of Uganda. However, legally, they might face difficulties in proving their Ugandan citizenship. This issue is also apparent among people of Rwandan descent, who have lived in Uganda for generations but whose citizenship status remains uncertain due to the changing borders of East Africa.

In Uganda, citizenship is also linked to nationality, but the two are not always identical. Nationality is often based on one's ethnic background and origins, while citizenship is a legal status conferred by the state. Many Ugandans of Indian descent, for instance, may possess Ugandan citizenship, but they might still see themselves as nationals of India. Likewise, a Dinka individual living in Australia could hold Australian citizenship but continue to identify as Dinka. This difference between legal citizenship and ethnic nationality offers a nuanced understanding of belonging in Uganda, reflecting the complexity of identity in a post-colonial state.

These tensions are especially clear when it comes to foundlings. This category could be exploited for political or social advantage. Abandoning a child to secure their citizenship by birth, whether in Uganda or another country, opens a pandora's box of legal and ethical issues. The easy granting of citizenship to foundlings, while shielding abandoned children, also risks creating an exploitative loophole.

The colonial legacy extends beyond just border rules. For ethnic groups like the Banyamulenge, who live near the borders of Uganda and the DRC, there are ongoing struggles with citizenship claims.

Despite their historical and ethnic ties to the region, these groups often find themselves excluded from full participation in Uganda's citizenship system because of their ethnic and geographical origins.

This dynamic between nationality and citizenship illustrates the wider tension between the modern state and its inhabitants. While Uganda must determine who its citizens are for governance and international relations, the borders established by colonial powers do not always match the true diversity and fluidity of identity in the region. The colonial legacy has resulted in a situation where ethnic ties that cross modern borders are not consistently recognised legally, leaving some individuals in a state of limbo. They may identify with a particular nationality, but their legal citizenship is often restricted or denied based on the borders imposed by colonial authorities.

Therefore, the issue of belonging in Uganda is complex. Citizenship laws, meant to manage membership in the nation-state, often do not fully account for ethnic, cultural, and historical identities. Uganda's current legal system needs to develop further to reflect the real experiences of its people and to better represent its diverse, multiethnic, and multiracial population, even if this involves addressing the legacy of colonial-era legal exclusions.

The discussion about Uganda's identity and its citizenship laws is undeniably intricate. It requires a careful balancing act between legal definitions, ethnic identities, colonial legacies, and the need for a progressive national outlook that embraces a shared future while managing the country's diversity. The questions raised here are less about straightforward legal definitions and more about broader themes of belonging, inclusion, and the moral responsibilities of citizenship.

In discussing Uganda's pursuit of greater regional integration, one cannot ignore the colonial legacy of fragmented territories. The movement for East African integration, as seen during Uganda's independence period, was initially hindered by regional kings and their desire to preserve their own power. This was especially evident in the case of the Buganda Kingdom, where King Mutesa I opposed the idea of ceding his kingdom to a broader East African federation. He understood that his people would lose significant control under the larger, British-created governance system. However, the realisation of East African integration could have had a transformative impact on the region by enabling countries to move beyond colonial borders and mentalities. President Nyerere of Tanzania was particularly forward-thinking in this respect, recognising the potential benefits of integration for economic, political, and social development. Although it did not unfold as planned, it remains an important point for reflection.

East African integration, which could have helped Uganda and its neighbours think beyond individual nationalistic interests, should remain an aim. The division of borders that was originally a result of colonialism no longer benefits the region. Countries like Uganda, Kenya, and Tanzania could gain from a wider, more regional outlook, one that emphasises shared interests, mobility, and opportunity rather than focusing only on inward-looking nationalism. The core message is about collaboration, not isolation. As Uganda faces issues of land scarcity, limited resources, and political tensions, regional cooperation, supported by shared infrastructure, trade agreements, and mobility, could offer new solutions.

Yet, despite the obstacles and historical tensions, the region continues to recognise the potential for a more integrated future. The drive for regional cooperation across East Africa is a call to move away from narrow, nationalistic views and consider the future of a connected continent.

From a citizenship perspective, this means not viewing one's identity solely through state-defined categories but embracing the shared history, culture, and potential. If Uganda, Kenya, Tanzania, Rwanda, and Burundi could find ways to remove artificial borders, it would open the door to greater opportunities, mobility, and shared prosperity.

However, as leaders consider these shifts in identity and regional cooperation, the importance of education cannot be overstated. Many of Uganda's challenges related to citizenship, belonging, and identity arise from ignorance, bias, and historical misinformation. As generations evolve, the young population must be educated not only about facts but also about the potential for a more inclusive, accepting, and outward-looking future. Education becomes the tool to combat the divisive tribalism that has historically been present in African societies, including Uganda. When people are educated and exposed to different cultures, ideas, and histories, the prejudices and assumptions that underpin much of the conflict can be reduced.

Exposure to diverse perspectives, histories, and the understanding that ethnicity should not define a person's character is a vital first step in breaking down the biases that still cause division. Education in Uganda should focus on promoting tolerance, mutual respect, and a shared sense of humanity.

In terms of citizenship, Uganda has considerable progress to make. The discussion about constitutional reform, especially within the context of a regionally integrated East Africa, must commence now. By the end of 2026, it will be vital to evaluate whether Uganda has achieved meaningful progress towards inclusion and integration or if it remains trapped in outdated paradigms. The urgency for a national and regional dialogue on how we perceive citizenship and identity has never been greater. The discussion must go beyond ethnicity and nationality, and centre on shared human dignity, fairness, and opportunity.

Reflection

In my conversations with Dr. Ruhweza, a constitutional law Don at Makerere University, I have observed that Uganda's citizenship laws stand at a crucial juncture. There is an increasing need to acknowledge the historical exclusion of certain ethnic groups, the complex nature of belonging across colonial borders, and the possibility of a new vision for East African integration. Uganda's future, as well as that of East Africa, depends on moving beyond a narrow, inwardly focused view of citizenship towards a broader understanding of shared identity and purpose.

I believe this will require us to intentionally dismantle colonial mentalities, to implement progressive policies, and to develop an educational system that promotes inclusivity. It will require thinking and recognising the potential for all citizens, regardless of ethnicity or birthplace, to thrive together in a united and integrated East African community.

My own journey in grappling with the question of who belongs and who does not has led me to uncover the biases and power structures that shape the concept of nationhood. I have also had to confront the quiet, often unspoken exclusions that persist within our communities—where some are considered more "nationalistic" and "citizen" than others, not because of law, but because of perception and prejudice.

It is now my firm belief that true citizenship must be rooted in dignity, inclusion and mutual respect. Citizenship should honour the spirit of Ubuntu, valuing each person's contribution to a nation's life, regardless of their background.

As we continue to redefine ourselves and our nations amid global migration, post-colonial legacies and shifting identities, the question must evolve from who belongs to how we can belong together. The purpose of nation-building can only be achieved through understanding who each person is.

The strength of knowing who we are must also then lead us to recognise and honour who others are, so that identity is not weaponised to divide, but used as a bridge toward a collective and hopeful future.

Chapter 7

Belonging...

To truly understand who we are, we must often look beyond the scripts handed down through tradition. Culture is indeed a powerful force. It shapes our language, customs, values, and even how we perceive ourselves and others. Yet, while it provides a sense of belonging and continuity, it can also become a cage that confines identity within inherited beliefs and practices.

This chapter was written to challenge to the idea that identity must always conform to legal, cultural and societal expectations. It invites us to examine the tension between personal truth and collective ideology. To go beyond the ideal norms is not to abandon one's roots; it is to seek deeper authenticity. In a world where culture can both nurture and restrict, how do we honour where we come from without being imprisoned by it? Here, I offer personal reflections, real-life experiences, and insights to help the reader grapple with this complex question and to awaken us to the power of knowing who we are beyond what we've been told to be.

Belonging and Culture

For a long time, I did not delve deeply into my own history. It seemed unnecessary. My focus was on the present, on surviving, building, and making sense of the life I was living.

My father occasionally mentioned Kasese, but only in passing. Mostly, he shared anecdotes about his childhood, the people, and the sights and sounds of the Rwenzori highlands. Occasionally, he would mention our great-grandfather's Yemeni roots, offering a brief glimpse into a distant past that was never fully explained. My mother, however, remained almost entirely silent about her ancestors. In our home, the past lingered like a ghost; present but never acknowledged.

That was probably why I kept that part of myself a mystery. It was not deliberate; I just didn't know where to start, and perhaps deep down, I was scared of the unknown, of what skeletons I might uncover in the closet and what they might mean. I felt more at ease creating my own story than digging up the old ones buried beneath layers of silence and forgotten time. As life went on and I faced moments that demanded more reflection, my curiosity increased. There was a stirring inside me, an almost spiritual hunger to understand: Who am I really? What hidden truths lie in the lives that came before mine? What does my history teach me? What patterns run through my lineage? More importantly, what lessons can I take from it in my own life today?

As I began tracing my genealogy, something remarkable happened. Certain patterns started to emerge. The first pattern I noticed was that my ancestors were not static people. They were movers, seekers, and pioneers in their own right. They crossed not only geographical borders but cultural ones as well. From Yemen to East Africa, from the coasts to the highlands, they journeyed with purpose, carrying a spirit of adaptability. They were not just wanderers; they were finders. They found opportunity where others saw uncertainty. They made homes in unfamiliar places, building bridges between cultures and communities.

Their lives reflected entrepreneurship, trade, and a profound sense of community responsibility. They were builders, not just of businesses, but of relationships, reputations, and legacies. They did not merely pass through places; they left lasting impressions that persisted long after their departure.

Their actions shaped the spaces they occupied, and their influence resonated across generations, even if names and specific stories faded with time.

This realisation changed my view. It felt as if a veil had been lifted. I no longer saw history as something distant or unimportant, just confined to dusty books or family tales. Neither was it something to be ashamed of but rather it was worth celebrating. I began to understand that history was alive within me. It was not only about what they had done; it was about what I was still doing, sometimes unconsciously continuing the same patterns they had started.

I began to recognise my impulses as echoes of those who came before me. I was not simply making decisions in a vacuum; I was standing on the shoulders of generations who, often through sheer grit, had carved paths that I now unknowingly follow. I realised that I am not the start of my story, but a chapter in a much longer book. With this realisation came both comfort and responsibility. I had to honour that lineage, learn from it, and add something valuable to the ongoing story.

However, this journey of self-discovery has not been without its struggles. Time and again, I have been confronted with a deeply unsettling question: Who am I? Am I Arab because of my adventurous Yemen ancestry? Or Comorian because of my maternal lineage? Or am I a Mukonzo due to my cultural upbringing and the soil on which my father was raised? I have often found myself suspended between these identities, fully embraced by none. I have been told, sometimes quite bluntly, that I am too dark-skinned to be Arab, as if complexion alone could disqualify someone's heritage. Conversely, my sharp features, nose, cheekbones, or hair texture, have prompted suggestions that I am somehow "not Ugandan enough," whatever that means. I do not blame them much however, because most times, we are always inclined towards what is familiar to us.

Even within the Bakonzo community, where I anticipated acceptance because of my father's heritage, I have occasionally faced subtle skepticism and quiet exclusion—questions about my lineage, whether I truly belong, or if I am merely an outsider disguised by cultural performance.

These conflicting signals, emanating both from within and outside the community, used to leave me in a state of limbo, constantly questioning not only my place in society but also the very framework through which we define identity in Uganda.

This personal crisis led me to revisit the very foundation of our nation's identity: the Constitution of Uganda. I started to analyse its language on citizenship, tribe, and belonging, seeking a mirror that could reflect my experience. Instead, I found a legal framework that, while seemingly inclusive on paper, often overlooks the complex and layered realities of people like me. I realised that identity in Uganda, much like in many post-colonial African states, is frequently reduced to rigid categories; tribes, regions, and races, leaving little space for the fluid, intersectional identities that many of us embody every day. By questioning the Constitution, I am also questioning society's capacity to fully recognise and accept the totality of who I am.

Belonging and the Law

A nation's Constitution aims to define who belongs, who is protected, and what rights are guaranteed to its people. As I examine Uganda's constitutional history, I cannot help but ask: Has our Constitution truly considered the diversity of those who call this nation home?

Uganda, like many post-colonial African nations, inherited governance structures mainly shaped by colonial rule. The legal frameworks imposed by the British overlooked the complex pre-existing systems of identity, belonging, and governance that African communities already possessed.

Instead, these colonial constitutions enforced strict classifications of citizenship, often favouring certain groups over others. Even after independence, the legacy of exclusion and categorisation continued.

One of the most notable examples of this was Idi Amin's expulsion of Asians in 1972. This sole event transformed Uganda's demographic and economic landscape. Essentially, it also raised a disturbing question: Who is a Ugandan? For those who had lived in Uganda for generations, built businesses, contributed to the economy, and called this country home, their citizenship was suddenly revoked. Their identity was called into question. While many of the misguided policies have since been revised, the repercussions of that decision still affect many multiracial Ugandans today, including myself.

If history has shown us anything, it is that exclusion does not merely affect those who are left out; it reverberates across every sphere of the nation. When any group is systematically denied a voice, opportunity, or visibility, the consequences are not confined to that group alone. Social cohesion weakens, trust in public institutions diminishes, and the nation's full potential remains untapped. Economically, politically, and morally, a society that sidelines segments of its population inevitably pays a heavy price.

The constitutional question, therefore, goes beyond just technicalities of legality or procedural correctness. It is mainly a question of justice, about whether all citizens are treated fairly. It concerns recognition, about whether every individual feels their identity, history, and dignity acknowledged within the national framework. Ultimately, it is a question of belonging—whether every citizen feels a genuine stake in the country's present and future.

A constitution that merely enshrines power without addressing these deeper human needs fails in its moral duty. To create a truly inclusive and resilient society, the law must not only set rules but also foster equity, healing, and shared purpose.

Belonging and Societal Expectations

Examining our Constitution today, I notice a significant and troubling gap in how identity is defined and recognised. It is a document meant to unify and govern all people under a single national identity. However, it falls short in recognising the stories of many Ugandans. In particular, the framework for tribal identification (one of the bases for defining citizenship and belonging in Uganda) fails to include people like me and many others whose families settled in this land during or even before colonial rule.

These were individuals and communities who, over generations, integrated into the social fabric, adopting local customs, languages, and livelihoods. Yet their descendants remain in a kind of legal and cultural limbo, citizens by presence, participation, and loyalty, but not by constitutional recognition.

This omission is more than a mere clerical error; it is a deep exclusion that leaves many individuals questioning their sense of belonging. When the highest law of the land fails to fully recognise their existence and history, it unintentionally casts them as eternal outsiders. They are people whose roots are denied, whose rights are questioned, and whose contributions are ignored.

As I reflect on Uganda's broader historical journey, I am increasingly convinced that most Ugandans, regardless of how extended their families have been here, are products of migration. Go back ten or more generations, and one will find that ancestors of many current ethnic groups moved across regions, settled in new territories, and established new communities. Even our myths and oral histories bear testimony to this.

The story of Kintu and Nambi, for instance, which is central to Buganda folklore, is ultimately a tale of migration and settlement. Similarly, the formation of kingdoms, chiefdoms, and clans throughout what is now Uganda happened through a series of movements (whether voluntary or

77

involuntary) long before the arrival of colonial powers and the drawing of arbitrary borders.

As a nation, however, we have failed to consistently confront this truth. We have romanticised certain identities and pathologised others, often drawing rigid boundaries around who is considered "indigenous" and who is not. This historical amnesia alienates many Ugandans and fosters exclusion.

It perpetuates a false narrative that some people are more Ugandan than others, a notion that contradicts the very essence of our collective history.

The constitutional silence on this matter is rooted, in part, in our colonial inheritance. The Ugandan Constitutional Conference held at Lancaster House in London from September 18th to October 9th, 1961, which preceded Uganda's independence, was dominated by a few voices, most of whom represented narrow regional or ethnic interests. Large swathes of the population, especially communities that did not neatly fit into the predefined tribal or territorial categories, were excluded from these deliberations. Their concerns and historical contexts were not given room in the emerging national structure.

The result? A post-colonial constitutional framework that prioritised consolidating state power in the central region and paid insufficient attention to the mosaic of identities across the land. This oversight has had long-lasting effects. It has left people disenfranchised and created divisions. It has also robbed Uganda of the chance to build a nation that celebrates rather than suppresses its diversity.

Had those fundamental discussions been more inclusive, we might have arrived at a different model; one that recognises identity not just through tribe, but through community, contribution, and history just as the cultural assimilation process had done for my family in Kasese. A model that accepts that Uganda is not a finished product handed down from colonial administrators, but a living, evolving nation shaped by migration, intermarriage, and shared aspirations.

Until we confront this reality and reflect it in our laws, the promise of unity in diversity will remain just that: an unfulfilled promise.

Redefining Belonging

Throughout this journey, one of the things that has stood out for me, is how kingdoms got it right by looking at the humanness or a person, most of the contemporary kingdoms and chiefdoms set the foundations right until the colonialists arrived and reset the tide.

Our Constitution, as it currently stands, contains notable omissions and oversights, especially in its failure to properly recognise and incorporate the traditional governance systems and cultural structures that existed in Uganda long before colonial rule. These indigenous systems, which played a vital role in community organisation, conflict resolution, and leadership, were either neglected or marginalised during the development of our post-independence legal and political frameworks. This exclusion has resulted in many communities feeling marginalised and unrecognised within the national fabric.

However, it is not too late to address these gaps. We have an opportunity and indeed a responsibility to revisit the foundations of our governance with a focus on inclusivity and justice. A truly representative legal framework should recognise Uganda's diverse cultures, languages, and belief systems. It must embrace the multiplicity of identities within the country, especially those that do not neatly fit into colonial-era or Western models of categorisation.

Understanding our past is not an exercise in nostalgia; it is a vital step in shaping a more equitable and united future. When we examine the origins of our current systems and consider what was lost or distorted, we empower ourselves to imagine and create something better. This book will act as a catalyst for such reflection, inspiring readers to explore their own heritage, ask difficult but necessary questions, and advocate for a national identity that genuinely reflects the diversity and dignity of all Ugandans.

The original Constitution may have fallen short of inclusivity, but we are not bound by its limitations. The process of nation-building continues, and we still possess the power to shape our legal and cultural landscape in a way that honours all voices and histories.

Living beyond cultural norms and beliefs doesn't mean rejecting our origins; instead, it involves carefully examining inherited narratives and asking: Which serve us, and which hinder us? Culture provides a foundation but not a limit. It offers a starting point, not a finish line. The journey of identity requires us to honour our roots while daring to pursue higher truths that affirm our individuality, dignity, and potential.

In the pages above, we have reflected how cultural beliefs can influence and sometimes constrain our sense of self. We have also observed the power that comes from questioning, reimagining, and redefining those norms when they no longer serve our purpose or growth. True identity is not limited by the expectations of a tribe, a tradition, or a past. It is uncovered in the space where courage meets truth.

As we move forward in this book, may we carry the lesson that identity is not a static inheritance but a living discovery. It is forged in the push and pull between who we were told to be and who we are becoming. And in choosing to live beyond the confines of culture, we give ourselves and, inadvertently, permit others to be fully, freely, and genuinely human.

G.B. ENGLAND. Heathrow Airport. Asians expelled from Uganda arrived, often penniless, at Heathrow Airport after being robbed by General Amin's soldiers and officials. 1972. (Credit: thebritishlibraryinstallation.com / © David Hurn/Magnum Photos)

Uganda's Independence. Conference, June 1962, Marlborough House. Reginald Maudling was then Secretary of State for the Colonies. (Credit: Jonathon L. Earle

Part III

IDENTITY: Hidden in Plain Sight

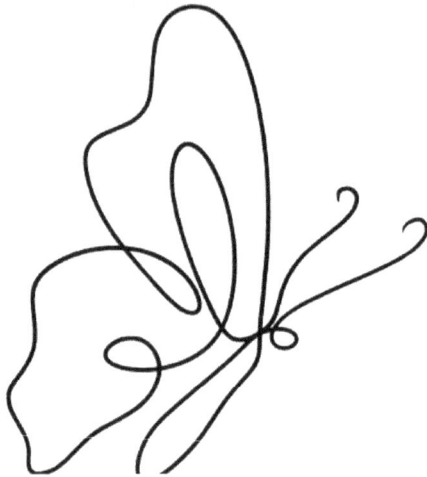

> *"To be yourself in a world that is constantly trying to make you something else is the greatest accomplishment."*
> *- Ralph Waldo Emerson.*

Race, religion, gender, and heritage have long shaped who we are and how others perceive us. This has created a tension between our self-identity and the labels imposed by the world. A detailed account of my identity journey, this section shares the experiences that mark milestones in uncovering my roots and embracing the power of my identity.

Chapter 8

A Mirror of Many Faces

It has been said many times that to truly know oneself is to confront the man (woman) in the mirror. But what if this proverbial mirror reflects more than one image? What if the reflection shifts depending on who is looking, from where, and with what expectations? In this chapter, I have chosen to explore the complex and often conflicting layers of who I am. Identity is not singular; it is a carefully mixed katogo (blend) of culture, history, language, faith, and gender. Like a mirror shattered into multiple pieces, each shard shows a different version of ourselves. Yet still, some versions we accept, some we resist, and others we have yet to discover

As I explored the forces that shaped my sense of self — gender, family, upbringing, society, and its experiences, I began to realise that identity is an ongoing dialogue between the individual and the world. This chapter encourages you to look more closely into your own mirror, to face the faces you present, and to consider how recognising each one is the start of freedom. As the Bible says in John 8:32, "And you will know the truth, and the truth will set you free."

When I was born, my father strongly wished to name me Zafaran in honour of his aunt. To him, the name symbolised a sense of legacy and respect, a way to preserve the family line. However, my mother was not fond of the name. To her, it didn't quite resonate. My uncle, who played a significant role in raising me and was always present in our home, agreed with her. He also found the name unsuitable. After some reflection, he suggested another name: Asmahaney.

My mother loved it immediately. She remembered that while she was pregnant with me, she flew with Kenya Airways on one of her travels. During that flight, heavily expectant and tired, she encountered an air hostess named Asmahaney. The woman went out of her way to care for her, offering a kindness that left a mark on my mother's heart.

Also around that same period, the wife of the ruling Sultan of Zanzibar bore a similar name – Asmahani. To my mother and uncle, the name now had dual symbolism: it was a tribute to a stranger's kindness and a nod to royalty. It felt elegant, rare, and dignified. To them, it held the essence of grace and strength, the kind of name they hoped I would grow into.

However, since my father still strongly preferred the name Zafaran, they decided to leave the final decision to a traditional naming ceremony. They wrote both names, Asmahaney and Zafaran, on pieces of paper, folded them carefully, and placed them into a small container. Then, in a moment that would define my identity, they gathered my relatives, cousins, and some neighbours to select one of the folded papers at random. The rules were simple: the name that appeared the most times after all the selections would be the one given to me.

After the draw, the results were tallied. Asmahaney had won. Just like that, the whimsical hand of fate chose my name.

In the early days of my life, I was a normal, healthy baby girl with chubby cheeks, bright eyes, and a zest for life. My mother often remembers those first months fondly, recalling how I would giggle endlessly, crawl around with boundless energy, and illuminate every room I entered. Things started to change when I was around two or three years old. Gradually, without warning, my health began to decline. The lively, plump child who used to fill the house with laughter gradually grew frail and bony.

My mother recalls that I was diagnosed with a heart-related condition. However, the details were never fully explained to me. What I vaguely remember is how the episodes would come in waves. During those times, I would suddenly lose weight, my once-thick hair would fall out in clumps, and I would grow visibly weak and lethargic. My energy would drain from me like a fading light.

This difficult chapter in my life coincided with a period of great upheaval for our family. We had to relocate to Kenya because of the political upset that characterised the 1980s. The tension in the region, coupled with uncertainty about safety and livelihood, made it impossible to settle in one place for long. While these frequent relocations may not have been the direct cause of my health issues, they certainly didn't help. The instability, stress, and lack of consistent medical care likely compounded the challenges we were already facing. Amidst the chaos of travel, border crossings, and temporary homes, my condition remained a quiet, ever-present concern.

It was in Kenya that I began my formal education, attending the Railway Kindergarten. My memories of that time are hazy, like fragments of a distant dream. Although time has softened the details, those early moments of curiosity and discovery still remain in my mind.

When we finally returned to Uganda, I resumed my early education at Kampala Kindergarten in Nakasero. The environment felt familiar yet different, and I was still learning to navigate the world beyond the comfort of my family. Not long after, in 1987, I enrolled at Buganda Road Primary School, where I would spend the next seven years of my life.

Buganda Road Primary School was more than just a school; it was a lively place, full of energy and character. It was a cultural melting pot where children from all walks of life gathered. The classrooms and playgrounds buzzed with children of various skin colours, hair textures, distant homelands, and unique accents. Many of my friends would often share stories about their home countries. Several of my siblings and cousins also passed through its gates, as did a wide circle of friends and classmates, each with a unique story shaped by different backgrounds, beliefs, and experiences.

Yet still, even amidst that rich diversity, I often felt different. I was conscious of an inner world that did not always reflect what was around me. It could be the way I perceived things, the questions I asked, or the silent struggles I bore. Whatever it was, it set me slightly apart. In that quiet difference, however, I also discovered the seeds of self-awareness. It was an early glimpse into the journey of discovering who I truly was.

I was a young girl who was just beginning to understand the world around her and my place in it. I was always afraid of speaking my views or addressing my curiosities because I was scared it would mark me as an outsider even more. Not only was I battling for my place in the world, but I had also just started understanding that the world can be cruel to a little girl who asks many questions.

Family, Identity, and the Complexity of Belonging

My upbringing was greatly shaped by the presence and wisdom of my maternal grandparents, particularly my maternal grandmother (a.k.a. Mpenzi, Swahili translation for Darling), who lived in the neighbourhood of Mengo. She was a steady, nurturing figure in my early years. Her home was a sanctuary where I always sought refuge. It was there that I learned the values of hard work, respect for elders, and courage, which influenced much of who I have become. Those early years with her shaped some of the foundational values I still hold even in my career to date. She was a woman who carried herself regally, perhaps partially owing to her noble roots. I always looked at her in admiration and awe of her strength and unquestionable grace.

During that same time, our immediate family lived on William Street, in the heart of Kampala. Our house, which had once belonged to an Asian family before the 1972 expulsion under Idi Amin's regime, stood directly opposite the William Street Mosque. The neighbourhood was always alive with activity; calls to prayer echoed through the air, the hustle of traders, and a stream of people weaving in and out of the city. It was an environment that kept you awake and engaged with the world around you.

Our home, much like the city itself, was full of life. Hospitality was not just something we did occasionally; it was part of our daily routine. We cooked as if expecting guests every day, and often, that was the case. My father strongly believed in the virtue of generosity. He taught us that shared food was never wasted, and an open door attracted both people and blessings. That mindset turned our household into something of a bed and breakfast or holiday inn; guests from far and near knew they would be received with open arms and a full plate.

Behind that lively and generous exterior, however, there was a quieter, more complex reality. My father, though a respected and charismatic man, was rarely consistently present. As a man with three wives and three separate households- ours on William Street, another in Najjanankumbi, and the third across the border in Kenya- his time was always divided. My mother was his second wife, and while she carried her role with the practised dignity and grace of a Muslim woman, the emotional and logistical demands of such a family arrangement were immense.

In the gaps left by my father's frequent absences, my uncles (my mother's brothers) stepped into the role of father figure. They were the ones who enforced discipline, offered counsel, and made sure we stayed on the right path. Whether it was escorting us to school, teaching us how to handle responsibility, or shielding us from the harsher realities of adulthood, they filled a crucial void. Their influence helped give structure to our days and security to our hearts.

Looking back, those years were a blend of contrasts: joy and longing, abundance and absence, simplicity and complexity. Throughout it all, the steadfast love of family, the richness of our cultural traditions, and the quiet sacrifices of those who filled the gaps made all the difference.

We grew up speaking Swahili, which reflected the Arab-Swahili cultural environment in which we were raised. This setting was rich in tradition, and polygamy was not only accepted but also celebrated. In our community, extended family and kinship ties were the bonds that held us together.

Our household was grounded in a collective sense of identity, shaped by values of respect for elders, hospitality, and a strong commitment to family loyalty.

My father, a man of quiet strength and commanding presence, did his best to foster unity among his many children. He made deliberate efforts to bridge the gaps that polygamy sometimes created. School holidays were carefully planned to bring all the children together under one roof. We were taught to see each other as one family. Although it wasn't always successful in bringing us closer, the effort made a difference, nonetheless.

Yet, despite his efforts to foster unity, I often found myself longing for something more personal: his presence. Not just his physical presence, but his attention, time, and undivided gaze. Even when he was nearby, he was often emotionally distant, his mind caught up in a web of obligations. He was a man in constant motion, hosting a steady flow of visitors: relatives, elders, neighbours, and community members, who came with needs, news, or simply the expectation of hospitality.

His open-door policy, while admirable and culturally expected, created an invisible barrier between us. It made our home feel like a public square, seldom quiet or private.

In that constant activity, I sometimes felt invisible, like a quiet voice in a crowded room. The house never seemed to stop, and in its endless rhythm, moments of intimacy were rare and fleeting. I learned to find comfort in silence, to draw reassurance from my siblings' presence, and to understand that love, in our world, was often demonstrated through duty and care rather than words or constant attention.

Every young girl longs to feel doted on, to feel seen, heard and understood. I was no exception. Even when her thoughts may seem naive or unpolished, a young girl still craves to be listened to. I don't think I expected more than my parents could give, but I have come to believe that for any girl to grow into a confident, bold woman, her father's affirmation and applause play a vital role.

That was missing for me. My father's absence created a quiet emptiness, one that I did not know how to fill. I found myself searching for that validation elsewhere, trying to mend a void that only seemed to grow bigger as I got older.

The Struggles of Being Different

Even as a young girl, I became painfully aware that I did not quite fit in, neither at home nor at school, and not even in front of a mirror. My complexion was noticeably darker than that of my siblings, a stark contrast that stood out sharply against the backdrop of our mixed heritage. While some of them had lighter skin tones and long, silky strands of hair that conformed neatly to society's standards of beauty, I had thick, coiled curls and deep brown skin that seemed to set me apart. In a world that often celebrated sameness over individuality and praised certain features as beautiful, my differences felt like flaws.

These physical distinctions did not go unnoticed. In fact, they were constantly pointed out, sometimes playfully but often insensitively. At home, my siblings would tease me mercilessly. They called me "skeleton," a nickname that lingered long after the illness that had stripped away my childhood weight had passed. At school, the questions from classmates came bluntly and without filter: "Why is she so dark-skinned compared to her sisters?" "Are you even from the same family?" The enquiries may have seemed harmless to some, but to me, they carried the weight of rejection.

Whether those comments were made in jest or out of genuine curiosity, they pierced deeply, nonetheless. They embedded themselves into my self-image, sowing seeds of doubt that grew into thorns of insecurity. By the time I turned twelve, I had fully internalised the belief that I was the odd one out—the ugly duckling in a pond full of swans.

I began to shrink into myself, constantly comparing myself to those around me and finding only inadequacy.

In response to this silent emotional turmoil, I adapted in the only way I knew how: I became a people-pleaser. If I couldn't be beautiful, I would be useful. I went out of my way to be kind, helpful, and agreeable. I would anticipate the needs of others before they even voiced them. I wanted to be liked, needed, and accepted. I believed that if I could not win people's admiration through appearance, then I would earn their affection through effort. My self-worth became tied to how much others approved of me. I found myself endlessly scanning faces for signs of approval, validation, even the slightest flicker of acceptance.

Looking back now, I realise that beneath that quest for belonging was a deep longing to be seen, not just for my appearance or what I could do for others, but for who I truly was. I wanted someone, anyone, to affirm that my dark skin was not a deficit, that my differences did not make me less deserving of love. In the absence of that affirmation, however, I learned to survive by becoming what I thought the world wanted me to be.

School became my refuge, a place where I could briefly escape the chaos and uncertainty of my personal life. Among all the subjects and activities, it was Music, Dance, and Drama (MDD) that called to me. On stage, I found a version of myself that felt brave, powerful, and unapologetically free. Performing allowed me to step out of the shadows of self-doubt and into a space where my voice, movements, and emotions could speak louder than my appearance ever could.

Each school performance and anticipated MDD competition was like a breath of fresh air, an affirmation that I had something valuable to offer. It was in those spotlighted moments that I felt truly seen and celebrated for who I was at my core. My mother, despite being a strict and no-nonsense woman, always made time to come and watch me perform. Her presence in the audience meant the world to me. They were small but significant gestures of support that fueled my passion and made me feel validated.

I was not alone in my love for the stage. I shared it with my childhood best friends, Aisha Namukasa and Patricia Kihembo. The joy, the laughter, the adrenaline—everything was part of a magical world where I did not have to pretend, compete, or explain myself. In that world, I was enough. For a child longing to be seen, that was everything.

A Forbidden Curiosity

Religion was another part of my life that was defined for me long before I could form my own beliefs. From as early as I can remember, Islam was not just a religion in our home; it was a way of life. We were raised Muslim, not as a matter of choice, but as a matter of identity. Every aspect of our upbringing was intertwined with the rituals and teachings of the faith. We attended madrassa regularly (an Islamic educational centre where we memorised the Qur'an), learned how to pray, and were taught the moral codes and obligations of being a good Muslim.

My father was particularly dedicated to making sure we stayed rooted in the faith. He took his responsibilities seriously and expected us to show the same level of devotion he did. Our household strictly followed the rules: prayers at set times, fasting during Ramadan, abstaining from what was considered haram (forbidden), and observing Islamic customs meticulously.

But even as a young girl, I felt restless in the face of doctrines I didn't understand. I had many questions that were rarely welcomed, let alone answered. Why couldn't women pray during their menstrual periods? Why were certain teachings considered sacred and immune to questioning? Why were we encouraged to obey rather than to understand? Above all, why did the burden of modesty seem to fall almost entirely on women and girls, with the expectation to veil, keep quiet, and submit?

My curiosity did not sit well with most of my teachers. In a system that rewarded compliance and punished inquiry, I was quickly labelled a troublemaker. Some of my questions were seen as signs of disrespect, even rebellion.

I remember the embarrassment of being singled out in front of the class or having my name mentioned at home with disapproval. Teachers reported me to my parents, accusing me of undermining their authority. I was not trying to be a rebel. I was trying to make sense of the world around me, of my faith, identity, and the place I was expected to occupy in it. Deep down, as I later realised, I was searching for a connection to God that felt real and not just inherited.

My first encounter with Christianity was through Kampala Pentecostal Church (KPC), now known as Watoto Church. I was a young pupil at Buganda Road Primary School, and one afternoon, a classmate enthusiastically invited me to attend a production called Heaven's Gates and Hell's Flames. It was a dramatic portrayal of salvation, life, death, and the afterlife. The invitation was spontaneous, and since it was free, I agreed to go along without hesitation.

I had never seen anything like it. The lights, the music, the intense emotion on stage, it all felt so real, almost too real. I was utterly captivated. Time ceased to exist for me in that moment. A whirlwind of thoughts and feelings consumed me I could not quite explain. For the first time, I found myself seriously contemplating eternity, God, and my own soul.

Meanwhile, our house help had come to school to pick me up as usual, only to find that I was nowhere in sight. Panic must have set in as he searched for me, wondering where I had vanished. Eventually, he traced me to the church, where I was still deeply engrossed in the scenes of the play. The relief on his face quickly turned into anger. When we got home, I was punished. In our household, any religion apart from Islam wasn't encouraged, and one had to follow certain unspoken boundaries.

That night, even as my body ached from the punishment, my heart was stirred in a way I could not describe. That evening at KPC marked both a beginning and an end. It was the first time I had truly stepped into a church, and for a long while afterwards, it would also be the last.

93

An invisible seed had been planted; something had been sown, nonetheless. Though I stayed away from church physically, the questions that experience awakened in me refused to go away. Who was this Jesus they spoke of with such urgency? Was heaven real? What about hell? Was faith meant to be feared or embraced?

In the years that followed, I kept wrestling silently with these thoughts. I yearned to understand faith, not as a tradition I was compelled to follow or reject, but as a personal truth I could find for myself. Deep down, I wanted to explore it on my own terms.

I think one of the things that drew me to the Christian faith, even at that young age, was that their God was not obscure. He invited questions. He was sovereign yet not threatened by curiosity or doubt. He was a God of freedom, and that was rare. I had never encountered any faith that portrayed God in this way.

As a young girl, all I longed for was the freedom to discover myself. The freedom to think, to create, and not to be confined by boxes chosen for me beforehand. I tasted that freedom. It was like taking the first sip of an elixir. I would later find myself returning for more.

The "Bachotala" Next Door

Growing up, I always knew we were different. It was not something anyone needed to spell out; it showed in stares, whispers, and awkward silences. People often called us *Bachotala*, a label that seemed to carry both curiosity and prejudice.

The term, loosely referring to our noticeably different hair texture and fairer complexions, made us stand out in a way that didn't always feel kind. We drew attention, not by choice, but because of the stark contrast to our peers.

At home, we primarily spoke Swahili and bits of English, languages that had become ingrained in our family's daily life. Luganda, the main local language, remained challenging for us. We understood it only in parts and spoke it cautiously, which made daily interactions with the wider community even more difficult. My mother, Riziki and grandmother Zena, however, often switched to Kinubi (a Sudanese dialect), especially when they wanted to keep their conversations private from our ears.

In our neighbourhood, we often felt like a spectacle, almost like characters from a foreign movie projected onto a Ugandan backdrop. Children would stare, whisper, giggle, and sometimes point openly, fascinated by our long, curly hair and unfamiliar facial features. It wasn't unusual for a few of the bolder ones to jump over our fence just to get a closer look at what they called "the kids with the long hair." It was both amusing and disturbing, like being animals in a zoo.

My father, a man of few words but strong convictions, did not take these intrusions lightly. He would storm outside the moment he heard the noise, his voice booming as he chased the children away. He wanted to shield us from the ridicule, the othering, the feeling of not belonging. But even he couldn't fully protect us from the weight of our difference.

That was our childhood reality, a mix of pride in who we were and confusion about how we fitted into the world around us. Being Bachotala meant carrying a dual identity, rooted in cultures that clashed as much as they coexisted, and learning from an early age that sometimes, being different came at a cost.

It made us feel like animals in a zoo, meant to be observed from afar, studied with curiosity, and quietly discussed, though never truly accepted as part of the scene. The stares weren't always hostile, but they carried weight. There was an impression that we were being watched rather than embraced. I remember hearing the word Bachotala whispered around us. At the time, I didn't fully understand its significance, but I could sense its sting.

It was not hurled at us with anger or contempt but spoken with a casual finality as if to say, 'You are not one of us.' It wasn't a slur in the loud, overt sense. Instead, it was a quiet branding, a constant reminder that we were outsiders.

That kind of subtle discrimination cuts deep. It slips into the cracks of your identity, making it harder to form a solid sense of belonging. You begin to question not only where you live, but who you are. At school, the questions came constantly, always in the same curious tone, but laced with skepticism: "Where are you from?" "What are you, exactly?" "Are you really Ugandan?" They were simple questions on the surface, but each one chipped away at the foundation of my self-worth. I would respond with quiet confidence, affirming my Ugandan identity, but the doubts lingered. I had the accent, I knew the language, I understood the customs. Somehow, that still wasn't enough.

I tried to anchor myself in the stories I grew up hearing, especially those about my grandfather. I remembered walking along the trails of Bwera during my rare visits, where locals still spoke of him with respect and affection. They shared stories of his generosity, integrity, and leadership. In those moments, I felt proud and validated. However, when I returned to my daily life, that pride often faded into confusion. How could I belong to a place that admired my family so much, yet still saw me as a stranger?

There was always a feeling of being caught in between, neither fully accepted nor completely rejected. That in-betweenness became the backdrop of my upbringing. I learned to read between the lines, to decode the glances, and to navigate the spaces where I was tolerated but not truly embraced. Although I never stopped believing I was Ugandan, I could not ignore the constant hum of difference that followed me. It was like a softly playing song in the background, easy to overlook at times, but impossible to entirely silence.

My father often told stories about Bwera, Bukonzo and its lush hills, the people, and the rhythms of life there. His memories stopped at his own father, never going further back into the past. He never spoke of his grandfather or the generations that came before. It was as if time itself began and ended with a single name, a single face. The rest often remained shrouded in silence.

Transitions and Defining My Path

When I sat for my Primary Leaving Examinations, I scored 12 points. It wasn't the worst outcome, but it wasn't outstanding either. I had long harboured a deep desire to join Nabisunsa Girls' School. In my mind, that school represented not just prestige but a place where talented girls thrived, and where I imagined, my dreams would begin to take flight. So, when the results were announced and I fell short of the required mark, I was crushed. It felt like a personal failure, a sign that perhaps I didn't have what it took.

For days, I grappled with a heavy heart and the fear of an uncertain future. Then, a ray of hope appeared when the father of one of my childhood friends, Aisha, who was the headteacher at Kibuli Secondary School, which was a co-ed boarding school, intervened. He extended a helping hand and facilitated my admission into Kibuli. Just like that, when all doors seemed to be closing, a new one swung open. It was not the path I had planned for myself or even wanted, but it turned out to be the turning point I never saw coming.

Arriving at Kibuli Secondary School, I carried a mixture of nerves and optimism with me. I was prepared to make the most of the opportunity and to prove myself. I entered the school expecting to keep my natural hair. My curls were more than just hair; they represented a part of my identity. Thick, springy, and unapologetically mine, they were an integral part of who I am. However, the moment I stepped onto the school grounds, that expectation shattered.

The school had strict grooming rules, and keeping my hair as it was, did not comply with the regulations. I was told I would have to shave it off, like everyone else. It might seem like a small matter, but to me, it was startling. The administration made it very clear: everyone, regardless of race, background, or personal circumstances, was required to cut their hair down to exactly one inch.

No exceptions, no negotiations. It was the school's way of enforcing uniformity. My father tried to reason with the staff. He explained that we had just arrived, the directive had taken us by surprise, and we hadn't had time to find a proper barber. The response was cold and mechanical. Rules were rules, and this institution, I was quickly learning, did not bend for anybody.

Lacking any other options, I was directed to a makeshift barbershop tucked away in a corner of the school grounds, where a *kinyozi*— a local, usually unskilled or semi-skilled barber—worked. Inside, a tired-looking old man barely acknowledged me before gesturing to a rickety stool. I sat down, heart pounding. He did not ask what style I wanted. He did not even speak. Instead, he simply grabbed his clippers and began hacking away at my hair like it was an unwanted weed.

I remember the cold metal of the clippers biting into my scalp. I remember the clumps of hair tumbling to the floor like fallen leaves. I remember how each lock that fell felt like a piece of me being erased. Tears rolled down my cheeks, silent and hot. I didn't resist; I just sat there, stunned.

When it was over, I glimpsed my reflection in a cracked mirror nailed to the wall. The girl staring back at me looked unfamiliar. My once carefully styled curls had turned into awkward, uneven patches. I barely recognised myself. It was devastating, not out of vanity, but because it felt like a harsh lesson in what it means to conform.

My father left shortly after. I watched him walk away, his figure growing smaller in the distance, as I prepared to face my new intimidating surroundings. I now had to confront the next challenge: moving into the dormitory, a place that would become my new home for the next few years, filled with unfamiliar faces, strict routines, and the silent demand to toughen up.

Kibuli's compound, perched atop a hill, greeted us with an intimidating presence. The school's elevated location gave it an almost majestic feel. Still, for a new student like me, everything about it felt overwhelming. Upon arrival, our luggage was handled by small metal trolleys, pushed by hired hands, and transported along narrow, winding paths that snaked across the hilly landscape.

As I followed behind the trolley carrying my suitcase, my heart thudded with anxiety. Along the path, clusters of older students had gathered, forming a daunting corridor of stares, whispers, and ridicule. They had come for one purpose: to size up the newcomers. For them, this was sport. For us, it was a nightmare. Every step felt like walking through a corridor of judgment. Their eyes scanned us as if we were creatures on display, and the mocking began almost immediately. Harsh, unkind laughter rang through the air, meant to bully us.

Eh! Look at that one!

"Nsolo!" they shouted, the word spat out.

The term "Nsolo," which literally means 'wild animal,' was their crude way of branding us new students. The hazing was ritualistic, a rite of passage that left many of us shaken and unsure.

Then came the nickname that hit me like a punch in the stomach: "Fat Bombola." I froze. The laughter that followed was deafening, and I could feel my cheeks burn with shame and anger. During my Primary Seven holiday, I had put on some weight. Now, it was being used as ammunition against me; my body became a spectacle for mockery. I felt humiliated. For a moment, I wished the earth would open up and swallow me whole.

Reaching the dormitory felt like emerging from a battlefield. I scanned the large room filled with metal double-decker beds until, to my relief, I spotted a few familiar faces of girls I had known from Buganda Road Primary School. Instinctively, we huddled together, forming a small island of familiarity in an otherwise strange and hostile sea. We chose a quiet corner of the dormitory and began setting up our space, careful to stay out of the way.

Our group was small, just a few of us compared to the numerous girls from Kibuli Demonstration Primary School, which was situated next to the secondary school. They seemed to know everything: the rules, routines, and even the nicknames of the teachers. They moved confidently and claimed the best spots in the dormitory without hesitation. In contrast, we were awkward, unsure, and clearly outsiders.

It did not take long for us to realise that we were at a social disadvantage. We did not speak their slang and were unaware of the unspoken rules. In their eyes, we didn't belong. Everything about our first day at Kibuli sent a clear message: survival here would require more than just good grades. It would demand strength, resilience, and, in time, a thick skin to withstand the insults we'd learn to endure.

Secondary school felt like a war zone at times. We were constantly tested, not just academically but emotionally and spiritually. It wasn't simply a place of learning; it was a battleground where identity, dignity, and justice were often under siege. Amid the chaos, however, it forced me to grow up quickly. I learned to navigate social power structures, to defend myself when no one else would, and to speak out when silence would have been easier. Those hallways taught me as much about courage as any classroom did.

One incident that remains vivid in my memory was an encounter with the prefect responsible for roll call during our daily morning prayers. On a particular morning, I hadn't attended the session. As I walked past, he stopped me with a stern voice, eyes already narrowed in suspicion.

"Why weren't you at prayers?" he demanded.

I took a breath and calmly explained, "I'm menstruating. I'm exempt from prayer during this time."

He looked at me for a moment, then sneered and asked mockingly, "For that long?" His tone oozed sarcasm and disbelief, as if I had fabricated my condition. Then, without hesitation, he threatened to punish me for skipping.

I refused. Firmly, I stood my ground and told him, with a steady voice despite the pounding in my chest, that he had no right to punish me.

He didn't take it well. He reported me to the school administration, trying to depict me as disobedient. The teachers also attempted to impose punishment, but I still stood my ground. From that day onwards, I was given a new label: rebel. I became known as the girl who pushed back, questioned authority, and was 'big-headed'.

Over time, I found myself drawn into more confrontations, not out of a desire for trouble, but because I could not stay quiet when I saw friends being unfairly punished, humiliated, or ignored. I spoke up, again and again, and each time, I felt a little stronger. A little more certain that my voice mattered. Secondary school didn't break me. It shaped me.

From a timid, mousy girl who never wanted to upset anyone and always sought to please others, I was now turning into an outspoken young lady who would no longer sit quietly in face of injustice. My friends started turning to me whenever they felt wronged, and time after time, I was called upon to speak on their behalf, to slay their Goliaths. A bold butterfly was beginning to crawl out of her cocoon.

Kibuli was not easy. It stripped me of comfort. It was a place where being different made you a target, and where silence could easily swallow your voice. Despite the hardship, Kibuli gave me something valuable I had not expected. It gave me a voice. It forced me to look inward and find a sense of self that didn't rely on external validation. It gave me the strength to push back when I felt diminished, to stand my ground when others tried to define me on their terms.

It was there that I first realised that survival sometimes means speaking out, even when your voice quivers. That silence, although safe, can be a prison. Yet, even as I learned to speak, to resist, the deeper questions about my identity never truly disappeared. They remained in quiet moments, in the spaces between laughter and pain, like a soft but persistent hum.

I remember watching other children confidently introduce themselves, tracing their family lines through generations with pride. Their identity seemed so anchored, so assured. I envied that sense of rootedness. For them, it was a birthright. For me, identity felt like a floating leaf, drifting wherever the wind carried it. I lacked the reference points that made others feel grounded. And when you do not fully understand who you are, it is easy to go through life feeling like an outsider, even when people surround you.

For many years, I kept those questions hidden. I pushed them to the back of my mind, hoping that ignoring them would somehow make them go away. I concentrated on surviving, fitting in, and being accepted. However, life has a strange way of bringing back the things you try to avoid. The very questions I had silenced started to surface again, stronger and more persistent.

Eventually, I could no longer outrun them. I had to confront the question that had quietly haunted me since childhood: Who am I? Not just in name, but in truth. That question became the turning point, marking the start of my journey. A voyage that would lead me into the depths of my history, through the confusing aspects of faith, and ultimately to the core of self-discovery. It would later reveal to me that identity is not always something you inherit; it is something you uncover, choose, and become.

Chapter 9

Life in the Saad Household

The Saad household was, in many respects, like any other typical family home; filled with laughter, youthful mischief, and the daily chaos that accompanies a full house. Ours was a uniquely lively and dynamic environment, shaped by extended family bonds and the polygamous structure of our lineage. My father, a man of considerable presence and influence, married three wives, and he fathered twenty children. His Kenyan wife had ten children, my own mother had six, and another wife, who lived in Najjanankumbi, had four.

This meant that at any moment, the house was filled with siblings, half-siblings, and cousins, each bringing their own energy, personalities, and drama. Our home was never silent; there was always a game in progress, a disagreement being resolved, or a shared joke echoing through the rooms. Yet beneath the warmth and family togetherness, there were occasional undercurrents of rivalry and tension.

As is common in polygamous families, issues of jealousy, competition, and perceived favouritism would occasionally surface, causing disputes and tension among the households. Whether it was about who received what from our father, who was spending more time with him, or whose needs were being prioritised, such tensions created a complex web of relationships that we all had to navigate from an early age.

Nevertheless, these challenges also fostered resilience within us. They taught us early how to live with differences, how to negotiate for attention and fairness, and how to stand firm when we felt ignored. In many ways, growing up in the Saad household was both a test and a training ground; one that prepared me for the harshness of the wider world.

My siblings and I shared remarkable harmony throughout most of our lives, connected not only by blood but by deep affection. We are six children in total, all born to our mother, and each of us has contributed in our own distinctive way to the family.

My sister, Hijira Saad, is the eldest among us. As the firstborn, she naturally took on the role of the 'deputy parent'. Hijira was the second-in-command after our mother, always stepping up to take charge in her absence. She possessed a commanding yet nurturing and reassuring presence. I admired her greatly as I grew up. Her strength, sense of responsibility, and unwavering devotion to our family set an example I often looked up to.

Following her was our second-born sister, Fadhila Saad. Fadhila had a gentle spirit and a contagious sense of humour. She was warm, playful, and easy to be around. I shared a special closeness with her. We were like companions enjoying the wonders and mysteries of childhood together. Her company was always a source of comfort and laughter.

Next in line was our only brother, Mohsen Saad, who later adopted our father's name, Mikidad, into his own—often affectionately shortened to "Mickey." He brought a lively energy into the household that was both spirited and endearing. Among all my siblings, I was close to Mickey. We shared more than just our age; we shared countless adventures that only he and I fully understood. Our bond built on deep trust and friendship, and to this day, it remains one of the most treasured relationships of my life.

I came after Mickey, then followed my younger sister Sumayah Saad, whose thoughtful nature and quiet strength added a much-needed voice of peace to the family dynamic. Last, but certainly not least, was our youngest sibling, Adill Saad—the baby of the family.

Growing up, we played together, learned together, and cared for one another. The older ones naturally looked after the younger ones, and our home was full of joy. This early closeness, built on shared memories and collective responsibility, laid a foundation of love and loyalty that still influences our relationships to date, even as adults.

Mickey and I

Mickey, as we fondly called him, was the third-born among the six of us, and the sibling closest to me in age. We shared a unique connection that words often failed to capture. Mickey was everything you could ever wish for in a big brother, supportive in the truest sense, endlessly fun, and full of boundless energy and spirit.

He had this magnetic presence that made people gravitate toward him, especially the girls, who absolutely adored his effortless charm. Behind that easy smile was a grounded, thoughtful soul. He was daring when he needed to be, never shying away from a challenge, and yet there was a softness to him that made you feel safe. He laughed loudly and loved deeply, and his sense of humour could lift even the darkest of moods.

Strong-willed and fiercely independent, Mickey had a quiet confidence about him, a kind of inner compass that guided him through life. Growing up in a family of four girls and just two boys, I often noticed that he bore the weight of responsibility as the eldest brother. The expectations placed upon him as one of the 'men in charge' were heavy, and I sensed that his way of coping was by adopting a laid-back, almost detached attitude. It was not indifference; it was a survival tactic.

His absence now feels like a void in the very rhythm of my life, but I carry his memory with gratitude. He taught me the importance of courage, the beauty of laughter, and the strength of simply being there for someone, even when you don't have all the answers.

As the only grown-up boy in the house (our youngest sibling, also a boy, was much younger), Mickey often sought comfort outside our immediate family. He gravitated towards our half-siblings and cousins, creating a sense of community wherever he could. He longed for that connection, that wider sense of belonging, and he found it outside the walls of our home.

This was a constant source of tension with our mother. Her parenting style was more protective, sometimes even controlling, perhaps driven by her desire to shield us from the darker aspects of growing up in a polygamous family. Accusations of witchcraft, mistreatment, favouritism, religious fanaticism, and various forms of abuse were common in our wider community. She did her best to protect us from all of it. But Mickey challenged those boundaries. Every holiday, he would find a way to escape, sometimes quite literally, and spend time in the homes where he felt free. This defiance strained his relationship with our mother. Yet, being the charmer he was, he always found a way to win her back, even if only for a while.

Mickey left Uganda around 2004, just before we graduated from university, to seek better opportunities in the United Kingdom. He settled there, and I never got the chance to see him again. We stayed in touch, but distance has a way of weakening connection, even between the closest siblings.

In October 2014, he broke the news that would shatter us; he had been diagnosed with stage 4 liver and lymphatic cancer. Less than a year later, on 22 May 2015, he passed away.

The months leading up to his death were some of the most harrowing our family ever faced. It would take an entire book to capture the details. Still, if I had to sum it up in one sentence, it was the loneliest, most painful, confusing, and traumatic season of my life.

We had drifted. Life had pulled us apart. He would call now and then, but in the whirlwind of my own life, there were moments I forgot to reach out to him entirely, and that truth carries its own weight. In my loneliness, I sometimes felt angry at him. Furious that he had left at the very peak of our journey, just after our parents' divorce. Enraged that he was not there. I believed he should have done more as the older brother. In moments of despair, I longed for his shoulder, but it was no longer within reach.

So, when he died, I struggled to accept it. I hadn't come to peace with how I felt about him while he was still alive. I had built up resentment and pain during his years away yet always held on to the belief that one day I would have the chance to talk and untangle the knot of feelings between us. His death stole that chance.

For a while, I lived in denial. Even after travelling with my older sister to the UK in November 2015 to visit his grave, it didn't bring the closure I had hoped for. He was buried there, in keeping with Muslim tradition. Because his family was there, I returned with my grief still tightly folded inside me.

I bore my pain silently. I went along with everyone else's emotions, adjusting so I could blend in. I buried the emotional trauma deep in my mind, telling myself I needed to move on. As a family, we never truly discussed his loss, whether knowingly or unknowingly. My father remained absent, while my mother, torn between religious beliefs and her own maternal grief, drifted emotionally in and out. What should have been a shared loss became a solitary wound.

Unbeknownst to me, this experience quietly developed into a troubled mental state as a result of extreme coping. My emotional trauma had hidden beneath the surface for years until the isolation and uncertainty of the COVID-19 pandemic brought it to light. In 2021, the shock of dealing with COVID -19 began to unravel the cracks within. Unknown to me the general anxiety level took a toll on my already fragile state of mind. I started to experience panic attacks, insomnia and extreme burnout. The self-drive to keep my law firm business a float, homeschooling my children, financial responsibilities as a caretaker of most of extended family and studies I was skilling up on in this same period nearly led me to a mental breakdown.

What seemed like an ordinary day in August of 2021 ended up with me on a hospital bed at UMC Victoria Hospital not far from my residence.

I checked in thinking I was experiencing a heart attack, later after many medical tests, the Doctor confirmed that I was experiencing some form of Post Traumatic Stress and referred me to psychotherapy and medication for the insomnia.

After a few sessions in psychotherapy, I realized mourning Mickey was one of the most painful chapters of my life. With no one to turn to, it became a matter between me, God, and receiving expert help. My parents' separation especially my father's absence and sudden exit from my life left so much pain that I had never dealt with. I had also gone through traumatic childbirth experiences due to an emergency c-section, starting a family in rejection and dealing with continuous personal relational issues. Literally a mix of unresolved traumas in my life (aka katogo) is what was brewing in me. With both professional and spiritual support, I began a healing journey with a new perspective in life. I had to find myself amidst all this chaos.

Today, I have found a place of peace. I carry my trauma as the fire that built me to become who I am today, a resilient woman just like women who came before me.

Taking off the Hijab

Growing up in a Muslim family with Arabic heritage, Islam was not merely presented as religion; it was life itself. Every action, word, and even thought was meant to orbit around the supremacy of God, revealed through Prophet Muhammad (SWT).

On the surface, these principles sounded noble and pure, yet the practice of faith inside my home felt less like spiritual devotion and more like submission to authority.

My father wielded religion as a shield, often using God's name to justify his decisions and silence dissent. My mother, in turn, used it as a tool of control, reinforcing obedience under the guise of holiness.

Certain phrases echoed constantly in our household: "Your path to Jannah lies beneath the feet of your mother," or "Your father is your god on this earth." These words were meant to inspire reverence, but in practice, they built a cage around me. I was trapped in a system where questioning my mother's decisions meant risking paradise, and failing to honor my father's authority was seen as blasphemy. There was no room for protest, or even for curiosity without the looming threat of being cursed.

As a girl, my body became another battlefield. Modesty was not framed as a choice; it was an obligation. I was dressed in coverings long before I understood what modesty even meant. The hijab was not presented as an expression of faith but as a command, one tied to fear: wear it or you will burn in hell. For years, I obeyed. But adolescence sharpened my sense of self. When I looked at my peers in school, hair out, skin uncovered, unburdened by the stifling heat under a hijab, I could not help but feel the sting of alienation. Why was I invisible? Why was my body seen as shameful, as something that needed constant hiding? When I asked, the answer was always the same: "It is religion." Yet I needed more than fear to guide me. I needed meaning, a place for me within this faith.

Eventually, I rebelled. Removing the hijab was not simply a matter of clothing; it was my first act of defiance, my first claim to my own body. It caused quarrels at home, accusations of disobedience and dishonor.

To me, it was survival. I was determined to escape the shackles that wanted to erase my sense of self. I have always had what I call a restless mind—the gift of asking questions no one wanted to answer. My father often sighed, exhausted by my "endless inquiries."

One memory stands out: I asked why every prayer in Islam had to be recited in Arabic. If God was universal, why was communication with Him limited to one language? Another time, during my menstrual cycle, I asked why I was barred from prayer or reading the Qur'an. "But that's when I need God the most," I told him. "Why would He turn away from me in the days I feel weakest?" The response was always a frustrated command to obey, never an explanation that met my hunger for understanding.

These moments shaped me. They taught me that my womanhood, in the framework presented at home, was treated as both sacred and silenced, revered yet restricted. My body, my voice, even my questions were constantly regulated under the weight of doctrine and fear. Yet deep down, I knew submission could not be the full story of faith.

Over time, I began to understand that identity is not a single mask we wear, nor a single rule we follow. It is a mirror with many faces, heritage, memory, culture, belief, rebellion, and hope, all colliding in a dance of contradictions and harmonies. To be a woman in this context was to carry both the weight of imposed silence and the fire of unyielding curiosity.

I learned that empowerment is not found in conforming to repressive rites but in naming them, questioning them, and daring to stand against them. It is in embracing every fragment of myself and weaving them into something whole.

To know oneself is not to erase the contradictions but to own them. It is to see clearly both where we come from and where we are determined to go. For me, true strength came when I stopped seeking permission to exist authentically.

It came when I realised that I could speak boldly, live honestly, and claim my place as a woman, no longer defined by fear, but by freedom.

Another significant transition that left a deep mark on my journey to identity was the separation of my parents. When they finally separated, it wasn't a shock to us. The cracks in their marriage had been visible for a while, arguments that lingered in the air, long silences that weighed heavier than words and a tension seemed to throb quietly within our home. What did surprise me however was the sudden emptiness that followed.

We went from seeing my father every so often to not at all. Communication dwindled to nothing. As children, we didn't fully understand the intricacies of their conflict or what it meant for us. All we knew was the familiar presence of a father, with its steady guidance and protection, was gone.

My mother was left to carry the weight of it all. Overnight, she became both mother and father, the steadying force who had to ensure that the rhythm of life went on. School fees had to be paid, meals prepared and our lives had to go on despite everything else.

She bore the brunt of responsibility with a grace that, at the time, I took for granted but later came to appreciate deeply.

In our community, educating girls was not something people fought for. Girls were seen as destined for marriage and domestic roles, their futures often clipped before they even had a chance to stretch out. My mother herself had been married at fifteen, before she could complete her secretarial course. The irony was not lost on me. She wanted me to live out the future she had not gotten the opportunity to have.

My father, to his credit, had always insisted on educating all his children, His stance was not born from a strong belief in gender equality, he did not express any belief that girls deserved the same opportunities as boys. He did understand the value of education, however and wanted his children to be educated because he knew what doors it could open.

Yet, when he left, he no longer enforced that conviction. The support waned and burden of our education rested solely on my mother's shoulders.

This is why my gratitude toward her runs so deep. She became the unyielding pillar that upheld our family, ensuring that no matter the odds, we would walk through the gates of school and push toward a good future,

Their separation did more than fracture our home, it fractured something within me, every little girl longs for her father's affirmation, to hear that she is seen, cherished and enough. That absence continues to carve at the hollow inside me, one that I had to fight tooth and nail to fill from within. I learned early to wrestle for affirmation inwardly, to validate myself when no fatherly voice was there to do it.

In the void, I clung to my brother Mickey. I followed him everywhere like a shadow. He became an anchor in the storm that had become our home. When he left for the UK and eventually died, I realised that my anchor was gone, and I started to drift. I felt alone, trying to hold on to a lifeline that was no longer there. I was drowning, trying to save myself by clasping at straws yet somehow sinking even deeper.

I felt lost, seen but not really seen. To others, I looked fine, but inside I was fading. I did not know where I belonged or who I was meant to be. I had tried to fit into what others expected of me, but it had only left me feeling emptier. I carried the quiet pain of someone trying to find herself again.

Chapter 10

Found in Purpose

Reclaim and Rise

The word 'reclamation' means that one is taking something back or reasserting a right. Reclaiming one's identity is a life-changing undertaking. One that demands courage, reflection, and resolve. Identity is not merely a label or an unchanging definition; it is a living, breathing thing that shapes how we see ourselves and how the world perceives us.

Yet, for many, this sense of self can be obscured, diminished, or even stolen by forces beyond their control, such as their history of oppression or current surroundings. In this chapter, "Found in Purpose," I call us forth to the battlefield. To confront the scars of the past and the chains that have held us captive. As I conclude the book, I want to awaken us to the power of knowing who we truly are beyond superficial narratives and external judgments. This will empower us to reclaim our dignity, rewrite our stories, and rise with renewed strength and purpose.

This is the transformative power of identity: not only to understand ourselves, but also to break free from limitations, to stand tall amidst adversity, and to shape a future.

This chapter is the heartbeat of my story, the reason I wrote this book, the reason I had to go through what I did, and why I continue to speak, search and share. It is my offering to you, the reader, as you trace the winding road of identity, belonging, and purpose alongside me.

This journey has not been straightforward. Like any path shaped by destiny, it has been filled with shadows and light, valleys and mountaintops. There have been countless moments when I felt lost, drifting in a world that demanded I be one thing while I knew I was becoming something entirely different. I was weighed down by many forces that tried to name me, define me, and confine me until I found my centre, Christ.

Finding Purpose in Christ

Christ found me in such deep brokenness. I had been walking through life burdened with pain, loneliness, and deep emotional wounds. I endured silently, always trying to present a strong face, but inside, I was just a shell of myself. During COVID, I was later diagnosed with minor mental health condition, but honestly, the cracks had been there all along.

Despite the trauma and everything I was going through, life was still moving forward. I got married in 2010. My firstborn arrived in 2011, and my second child was born in 2013.

I was embarking on this new journey with my husband, raising a young family without my parents' support. By the time my wedding took place, my parents had cut ties with me because of my decision to marry a Christian.

That decision shattered the inner child in me. It left me feeling completely abandoned. Because of the early scars I had already carried, I felt that my parents had never truly been there for me in the moments I needed them most. When it came to such a massive milestone in my life, I expected support, but instead, they made demands.

They asked that my fiancé should become either Muslim or else I would have to find someone else who was 'religiously aligned'. I could not hear them clearly. All I saw was entitlement to a life they had not been entirely part of.

Ultimately, I decided to follow my own path. Throughout my life, I felt like I was on a lonely journey, with only my siblings and friends to support me, never really my parents. Making this decision hurt me even more, but I pressed on with the wedding. We had a beautiful wedding at Serena Hotel Kigo, which had just opened at the time. Friends supported us. It was a small but lovely civil wedding. From there, we began our life together. I later had my children, but even in the joy of motherhood, I still carried pain and loneliness in my heart.

My career kicked off as I moved from corporate jobs into international organisations. The grace of God was sufficient, and we were not doing badly as a family. We were a young couple struggling to find our footing, raising little children without the support of my parents, relying only on God's grace, friends, and a small circle of kin.

Much of the weight was on us, and I carried much of it personally. It was troublesome, but I kept navigating through it.

Because of what happened with my parents and how religion was used to claim control my life, I rejected Islam. I felt it was unfair that religion had replaced my parents' love. We decided that our children should have the freedom to choose. When they became adults, they could decide for themselves whether to be Muslim or Protestant, since my husband was Protestant. Instead, while they were growing up, we would raise them simply as good human beings.

My philosophy became to raise them with kindness and love, without boundaries or restrictions. I wanted them to grow with joy and to discover their own identities as they grew older.

I carried a conviction not to bind them into any boxes that would imprison their sense of identity, not even religion. This became the doctrine by which I raised my children. Life went on in this way. I did not go to the mosque, and my husband did not go to church. We were simply living and navigating life as best as we could.

Later, I secured an excellent job with an international oil and gas company. It was my second international position, following my initial experience in telecommunications. My husband was also growing his business. On the surface, life appeared stable. But pain is pain. Pain without identity, pain without self-awareness, and trauma that is simply set aside do not just go away.

After my second child in 2013, I experienced postnatal depression. At the time, I did not understand what it was, but I recognised it later when I began to address my mental health challenges following the pandemic. The depression after childbirth was one of the early signs. Because I had C-section deliveries, I suffered from the aftereffects of anesthesia. I experienced spinal pain, persistent headaches, and overall weakness. The physical pain led to emotional pain. I hated myself and my body because I had gained a lot of weight. I quickly sank into deep depression.

Yet I could not show it. I wore a cheerful mask for the world. I always tried to appear happy, but inside, I was hurting deeply. It reminded me of my childhood, when I was silently carrying wounds while pretending to be fine.

Amidst this brokenness, God began to reach me through the people He placed in my life. My sister Fadhila had already found her way to Christ and often spoke to me about her healing. Whenever we met, she shared pieces of her journey with me, and I listened, even if quietly. Around the same time, my friend from the oil and gas company, Natasha Nakimuli Mulumba (Nalongo), became a true destiny helper. We started out simply as colleagues, but she soon grew into a sister and a strong pillar in my life.

Natasha invited me to church and different fellowships she was part of, but I was hesitant because of the emotional scars Islam had left in me. I was not ready to explore God in any new form.

Natasha gradually walked alongside me. She presented me with my first Bible as a gift. She told me, "Whenever you feel lost, just read a chapter." Being someone who loved reading, I took her advice seriously. Out of curiosity, I began to read. I started asking her questions. She introduced me to teachings by Joyce Meyer and T.D. Jakes, and it became a daily habit for me to listen to one or two teachings.

Joyce Meyer's story, in particular, resonated with me because of the candid discussion of healing and brokenness. I began listening to her daily. The first book of hers that I read was "Battlefield of the Mind." It touched my heart in a way few things ever had. Nevertheless, the guilt from my upbringing in a Muslim family weighed heavily on me. The boundaries and rules I had grown up with were so deeply ingrained that I couldn't see myself surrendering to Christ fully.

Until 22nd October 2016.

That day, Natasha invited me to a women's breakfast at the House of Revival Church. At first, I declined. I didn't want to go to church. She persisted and even paid for me. Out of guilt and her insistence, I finally agreed. At the breakfast, the keynote speaker was Dr. Tony Hasahya. He preached about foundations, family, and brokenness. His message struck me deeply. As he spoke, I broke down and cried. He described my life in ways I had never voiced aloud.

At the end, he made an altar call. He said he knew there were people in the room who were broken and needed Christ. I knew I was one of them. I walked forward first. I held his hands and said, "I am ready to give my life to Christ." That moment marked the beginning of my new journey. From then on, the House of Revival became my family. Coming from an Islamic background, they embraced me with love and recognised my brokenness. For the first time, I found a spiritual home. I dedicated myself to the journey of faith, seeking healing and my identity.

I started realising that my identity was not in my past, my pain, or the stories spoken over me. My identity had been established by God even before I was born. Christ gave me purpose and meaning. My first task was to uncover who I truly was. I began a journey of self-discovery in Him.

Since 2016, I have been on this journey. It has not been without difficulties. Crises are inevitable, even in Christ, but I have learned that faith is not about perfection; it is about transformation. It is about allowing God to reveal purpose through every crack and wound and letting His light shine even in places I once thought were too broken to matter.

Through Christ, I found my voice. As a woman, my voice had often been stifled by culture, expectation, and fear. But in Him, I began to speak differently. I began to see my gifts, my vision, and my courage rise to the surface. I discovered that I was not only a survivor but a builder—a woman who could create, nurture, and raise communities. I realised that my brokenness no longer defines me, He does. Through Him, I found healing, identity, and the permission to stand in the fullness of who I am. In Christ, I learned that my worth was not tethered to how obedient, silent, or useful I appeared to others, but to the truth that I was crafted in God's image. My strength, my emotions, my scars, all of them found meaning in Him.

Finding purpose in God transformed everything for me. He revealed that I am not defined by the names others called me, by the failures I carried, or even by the dysfunctions I was born into. Trauma and brokenness no longer set the boundaries of my identity.

In Him, I found clarity, power, and truth. I got the courage to turn away from the labels that had been placed upon me.

It taught me that identity, like the universe, must revolve around a centre. When the centre is strong, everything else begins to orbit in harmony. Just as the Earth moves with order around the sun, our lives find rhythm and purpose when anchored in God. For me, that unshakeable centre was Christ.

And it was from that centre that my search deepened. I began not only to trace myself spiritually but also genealogically. I dug into my lineage, into the stories buried beneath time, and what I found amazed me: royalty, migration, courage, and enterprise. I discovered a line of leaders, women and men who carried both scars and strength. Suddenly, my boldness and my unrelenting drive to build, to nurture, to lead all began to make sense. These qualities were not accidents; they were inheritance. They were intertwined in the strands of my DNA.

As a woman, this discovery was especially profound. For generations, women in my family carried resilience quietly, often in the background, holding households together, passing down wisdom in whispers. In Christ however, I realised that their sacrifices and strength were not just survival; they were seeds. I am their fruit, living proof that they endured for a reason, that their courage flows into me and through me. My existence is part of their legacy.

Every one of us carries something sacred in our bloodline. Every woman and man walking this earth carries a story that deserves to be named, a legacy waiting to be uncovered, and a purpose longing to be lived.

The difference lies in whether we will search for it, dare to embrace it, and dig beyond what has been handed to us to reach what God has promised.

God has always worked through lineage, families, and generations. The Bible itself begins with genealogy. Matthew traces the lineage of Jesus across 42 generations, clearly showing that God does not bless in isolation, but through continuity. As a woman in Christ, I now see my identity as both a personal awakening and a generational assignment. I am not just one story but many.

Rise

This is the core of my call to action: Know your roots, find your centre, and rise. As individuals, communities, and nations, we must remove the scales from our eyes and truly see each other. Recognise the human story in all of us. Understand that none of us have reached where we are alone. Uganda itself is a nation of many nations. Borders were drawn, not born. Our ancestors crossed lands that today have different names, but the blood in our veins tells a more united story.

Let us become a people who value community not just in words, but in practice. We should be seekers of truth, history, and belonging. We must question the social, legal, and political systems that have alienated so many, and rebuild them with empathy and justice. We must teach our children to ask questions, to discover, and to hold fast to their centre.

I want this book to transcend its pages. I want it to be read in schools, in government institutions, in immigration offices, and at border posts.

I hope it sparks conversations, helping a nation remember that we are not strangers to one another but relatives, separated by history and now reunited through truth.

This is how national transformation begins: through individual healing, personal understanding, and collective remembrance. The baton has been passed to us; let us not waste it. Let us remember our true identity. We must reclaim our roots and rise into what we are becoming—our power.

Reclaiming our identity awakens a power within. A power rooted not in external validation but in the truth of who we are. It is a brave act of remembering, healing, and embracing the fullness of our history, our struggles, and our triumphs. When we reclaim what was taken, overlooked, or diminished, we break the chains of limitation and rewrite the narrative of our lives.

Where has this journey of identity led me? What I have I picked from knowing my ancestry? I am sure you must be wondering. Well, the simple answer is this.

When I look back, I see the threads that have quietly shaped who I am today. From my ancestors, I have inherited the courage to face uncertainty with steady resolve. I have inherited the heart of service that causes me to show up for others and give hope where it is needed, as well as a deeply ingrained sense of community. These are not just stories of my past now; they live on in me now. They show up in how I love, lead, create, and what I believe.

Each of us carries something special from those who came before us. Perhaps it is wisdom, kindness or vision. Whatever it is, it becomes our quiet inheritance, urging us to pause and ask: What have I received from my lineage, and how am I honouring it?

For me, purpose was found in God. It is in Him that my identity anchored and my steps gained direction. He became the source, the breath, and the guide that turned my questions and burdens into fuel for growth. Yet I know this may not be the path for everyone, and that is okay.

Purpose can take many forms, but there are a few simple truths that can guide anyone searching for it.

- Step 1- *Seek Your Center- Find what grounds you, what gives you stability in the midst of life's storms. For me it was my newfound faith in Christ.*

- Step 2: *Turn your burdens into fuel- The questions, the struggles, and losses you carry can become the energy that propels you. - For me the burden of loneliness in family, dysfunctionality and early maturity built a character of resilience.*

- Step 3- *Observe your character- Pay attention to who you are when no one is watching; integrity is a compass. - Your personality is unique to you and self-awareness is the greatest guide to finding purpose.*

- Step 4- *Ask what you can change- Purpose grows in action, in how you impact the world around you. It is never about you. For me writing this book and its impact in the world is a great testimony of my purpose.*

To know who you are is to stand on solid ground. But to live with purpose is to rise, to move beyond yourself, and to let your life speak, Identity anchors us, but purpose propels us. It is the horizon that beckons, the fire that shapes and refines us, and the path that turns survival into meaning.

In conclusion, as I share my life's journey, it is impossible to capture it in a single story. My experiences are too layered, too intertwined, and too expansive to be contained in one book. They form a trilogy, and this book is the first of the three.

My journey is a trilogy of becoming, and this first book lays the foundation of identity and belonging. The next book will carry you further into the waters of courage, where we will explore what it means to rise, to take risks, and to step boldly into the life we are meant to live.

Saad Sayyid
Paternal Grandfather

Zena and Abdalla Katende
my maternal Grand Parents.

Nuru Talibali
My grand Auntie
Maternal

Haji Mikidad Saad Bin Sayyid
Author's Father

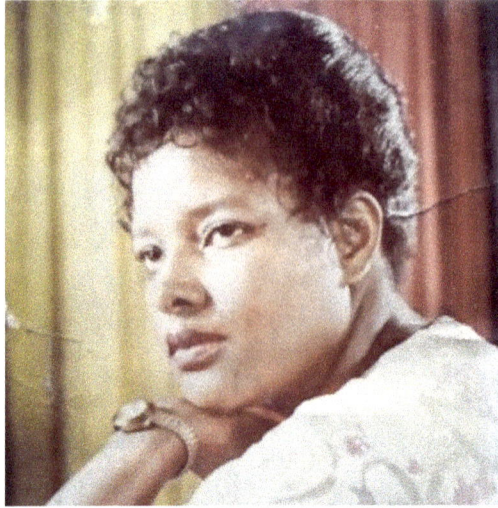

Hajati Riziki Abdalla Fumu Katende
Author's Mother

Author's Family picture

*The Late Mohsen Mikidad Saad
aka Mickey, my beloved brother*

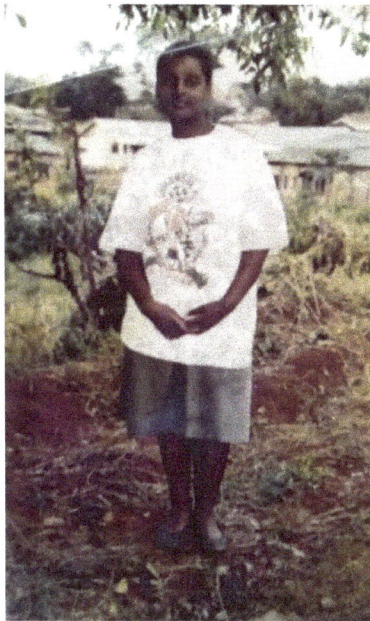

Author, as a young girl in

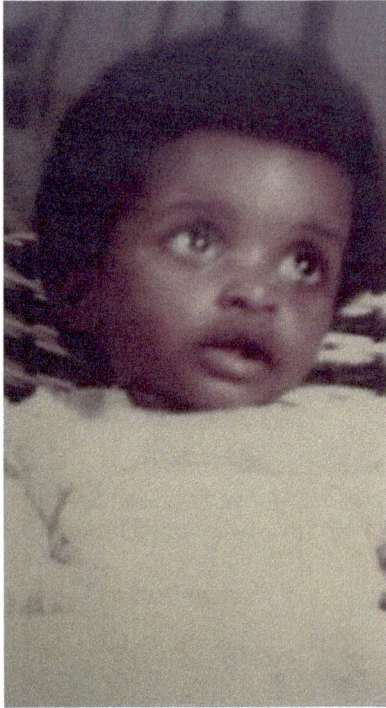

Author as a baby

Worksheets and Appendices

REFLECTIVE JOURNAL PROMPTS

This worksheet provides a prompt to help you reflect on each chapter of the book and identify your key learnings or main takeaway.

"This ordeal reaffirmed my determination to advocate for myself and others facing racial or ethnic profiling."

Prompt:

Recall a moment when your identity was questioned or misunderstood. How did it make you feel? What did you learn about yourself through that experience?

_____

_____

_____

_____

_____

_____

Chapter 1 – Saad- The Beginning

"It is in these roots that I found both identity and the resolve to rise above prejudice."

Prompt

What stories or values have been handed down through your paternal line? In what ways have they influenced how you navigate your life today?

_____

_____

_____

_____

_____

_____

_____

_____

_____

_____

Chapter 2 – The Matriarch's Thread

"We are descendants of warriors, scholars, healers, and royalty."

Prompt

Reflect on the women in your maternal line. What strengths or traditions have you inherited from them?

_____

_____

_____

_____

_____

_____

_____

_____

_____

_____

Chapter 3 – Connecting the Dots: How My Parents Met

"Their marriage in the 1970s sealed a union between two powerful traditions."

Prompt

Which aspects of your parents' relationship or cultural backgrounds have shaped your sense of identity or how you feel your place in your community?

_____

_____

_____

_____

_____

_____

_____

_____

_____

Chapter 4 – The Land, The People and The Name

"Migration came with many advantages but also brought profound struggles."

Prompt

Has your family gone through migration or resettlement? What opportunities or tensions resulted from that move?

_____

_____

_____

_____

_____

_____

_____

_____

_____

_____

_____

Chapter 5 – The Making or Breaking of a Nation

"Citizenship was reduced to a matter of ethnic and racial identity."

Prompt

Have you or someone you know ever been made to feel like a stranger in your own country or community? How did that influence your sense of belonging?

_____

_____

_____

_____

_____

_____

_____

_____

_____

_____

Chapter 6: Uganda - A Nation of Many Faces

"Citizenship laws often fail to capture the full complexity of ethnic, cultural, and historical identity."

Prompt

Do you feel completely recognised and represented by the laws and systems of your country? Provide reasons for your answer.

_____

_____

_____

_____

_____

_____

_____

_____

_____

_____

Chapter 7 – Belonging...

"I no longer saw history as something detached from me, but something living within me."

Prompt

How much do you know about citizenship and the laws related to belonging?

_____

_____

_____

_____

_____

_____

_____

_____

_____

_____

Chapter 8 – A Mirror of Many Faces

"If you do not fully understand who you are, you move through life feeling unanchored."

Prompt

When did you first realise you were "different" in some way? How did that influence your self-image while growing up?

_____

_____

_____

_____

_____

_____

_____

_____

_____

_____

Chapter 9 - Life in the Saad Household

"In many ways, growing up in the Saad household was both a test and a training ground."

Prompt

How has growing up with your siblings and immediate family affected your sense of identity?

_____

_____

_____

_____

_____

_____

_____

_____

_____

_____

Chapter 10 - Found in Purpose; Reclaim and Rise

"Understanding our past is crucial for shaping our future."

Prompt

What is one step you can take this month to reconnect with your roots, educate others, or advocate for inclusion in your community?

_____

_____

_____

_____

_____

_____

_____

_____

_____

_____

_____

BEFORE & AFTER REFLECTION WORKSHEET

Section A: Before Reading

Reflect on your mindset and understanding before you started reading this book.

Reflection Area

How strong is your connection to your ancestry or roots?

_____

_____

_____

_____

What do you know about your family history?

_____

_____

_____

_____

How do you describe your sense of identity?

_____

_____

_____

_____

Have you ever questioned your sense of belonging within your country or community?

_____

_____

_____

_____

What does citizenship mean to you, legally, emotionally, and culturally?

_____

_____

_____

_____

How do you perceive people from mixed heritage or immigrant backgrounds?

_____

_____

_____

_____

SECTION B: AFTER READING

Now that you've read: **Identity: Lost in History, Found in Purpose**

Consider how your perspective has changed.

Reflection Areas

How has your perception of identity evolved?

_____

_____

_____

_____

Which aspect of your personal or family history are you now interested in exploring?

_____

_____

_____

_____

What is one belief or assumption you now view differently?

_____

_____

_____

_____

How has the book changed the way you view others whose identity is complex or often misunderstood?

_____

_____

_____

_____

What practical steps will you take to preserve, learn about, or pass on your heritage?

_____

_____

_____

_____

What message or theme from the book will stay with you the most? Why?

_____

_____

_____

_____

Final Reflections

In one sentence, finish this thought:

After reading this book, I now understand that identity is

_____

_____

_____

_____

After reading this book, I now understand that power is rooted in

_____

_____

_____

_____

www.ingramcontent.com/pod-product-compliance
Lightning Source LLC
Chambersburg PA
CBHW071223090426
42736CB00014B/2952